The True Sto

BLACK PEOPLE CAN'T SWIM

Finding the Faith to Defy Your Odds

DAMONE BROWN

First Hardback and Paperback Editions

Some names, businesses, places, events, locales, incidents, and identifying details inside this book have been changed to protect the privacy of individuals.

Bible version used:

The Holy Bible, English Standard Version. ESV® Text Edition: 2016. Copyright © 2001 by Crossway Bibles, a publishing ministry of Good News Publishers.

Published by Freiling Agency, LLC.

P.O. Box 1264
Warrenton, VA 20188

www.FreilingAgency.com

HB ISBN: 978-1-963701-03-6
PB ISBN: 978-1-963701-04-3

E-book ISBN: 978-1-963701-05-0

TABLE OF CONTENTS

DISTURB US, LORD

Disturb us, Lord, when
We are too well pleased with ourselves,
When our dreams have come true
Because we have dreamed too little,
When we arrived safely
Because we sailed too close to the shore.

Disturb us, Lord, when
With the abundance of things we possess
We have lost our thirst
For the waters of life;
Having fallen in love with life,
We have ceased to dream of eternity
And in our efforts to build a new earth,
We have allowed our vision
Of the new Heaven to dim.

Disturb us, Lord, to dare more boldly,
To venture on wider seas
Where storms will show your mastery;
Where losing sight of land,
We shall find the stars.

We ask You to push back
The horizons of our hopes;
And to push into the future
In strength, courage, hope, and love.
This we ask in the name of our Captain,
who is Jesus Christ.
—*Sir Francis Drake –1577*

FOREWORD

My dad, Sergeant Major Walter Shumate, and a handful of Green Berets created the Special Forces Underwater Operations (SFUWO) – SCUBA School in Key West, Florida, in 1964. Growing up around Special Forces motivated me as a young man to become a Green Beret and make the Army a career. As a young Captain, I was fortunate to complete SFUWO's challenging Combat Diver Qualification Course (CDQC) and later serve as the Commander for SFOD-A 775. Combat Dive Team 775 has a rich history in the 7th Special Forces Group (Airborne) and in combat.

My father and I were both blessed to have successful 30-year active-duty Army careers, with the majority of our service time in Special Operations units. Despite serving in different eras, it was rare to know a SF Combat Diver that was an African American. Prior to meeting Damone, I only knew one black Combat Diver. Why was that? Could it be true that black people can't swim? I don't think so.

Damone Brown overcame the obstacles associated with becoming a Green Beret and continued to challenge himself by volunteering to serve on Special Forces Operational Detachment – Alpha 775 (SFOD-A 775), the primary Combat Dive Team in

3rd Battalion, 7th Special Forces Group (Airborne) since the early 1990s. As a young SF Engineer Sergeant, Damone was assigned to the Battalion as it was transitioning out of Latin American operations and beginning regular combat deployments to Afghanistan. Alpha Company, 3/7th SFG(A), and SFOD-A 775 saw extensive combat over the next fifteen years. They suffered casualties and lost teammates on these deployments as they continued their SF combat missions in Afghanistan.

Despite being in different Companies in the 7th SFG(A) in 2006, Damone and I deployed to Eastern Afghanistan at the same time but stationed in separate locations. He quickly became known as a quality SF Non-Commissioned Officer in A/3/7th SFG(A). After returning from that deployment, Damone set his sights on completing Pre-SCUBA and graduating from CDQC. He would not quit until he had earned his Combat Dive badge and a permanent position on his Special Forces SCUBA Team. Damone overcame all the challenges, obstacles, and naysayers in front of him to become an extremely successful Special Forces Combat Diver and conducted four combat deployments with SFOD-A 775 and the 7th SFG(A) to Afghanistan.

Black People Can't Swim will inspire future US military personnel and American citizens to overcome whatever challenges and hardships they will encounter in life. Damone is the only Chaplain's Assistant that I ever knew who went on to become a Green Beret. He is still only one of a handful of African American SF Combat Divers that I know.

Damone's life story will reinforce why you must be bold to explore new depths and distances. His journey will illustrate that the only way to really achieve your goals and greatness in this world is to lose sight of the shore and not be afraid to go for it in life. Quitting is not an option.

Damone's faith in God has served him well, both in the past and today. Like Damone, God wants you to go for it and to be all that you can be! Damone and his loving family continue to inspire those around them to "go for it" in life and "to never quit," regardless of the challenges you may face.

It is my honor to write these words about Damone Brown and his inspiring book *Black People Can't Swim, Finding the Faith to Defy Your Odds.*

—Colonel (Retired) Alan Shumate,
US Army Special Forces – Combat Diver

ACKNOWLEDGMENTS

I have the deepest gratitude to my wife, Marleanda, who has believed in me in those times when I didn't believe in myself and has stayed by my side through my best times, but more importantly through my worst. Being a Special Forces wife is not for the fainthearted. I am grateful to have you as my partner in trusting in God's "precious and very great promises" (2 Peter 1:4). Thank you for your gracefulness by which you do life with me. You are a daily reminder of the depths of God's grace and mercy, neither of which I deserve.

Thank you to my mother and father. I am the man I am today because of your love towards me. Through your lives, I was given my greatest attribute—my faith in God.

I am grateful to my children who encourage me more than they will ever know. Each of you are gifts from God. May the work of your hands surpass your limited ability to dream and may each day of your lives reflect your purpose, to glorify God.

"Have you ever wanted to do something big, but been told that you can't for whatever reason?"

INTRODUCTION

When I joined the Army in 2002, my mom, a full-bird colonel in the US Air Force at the time, sent me an article from the *Washington Post* that revealed a staggering statistic that only 2 percent of US Army Special Forces were black. Ten years later, the numbers are still shocking. A 2015 *USA Today* article reports that African Americans made up 17 percent of the 1.3 million-member Armed Forces in 2013, but of that 17 percent, eight of 753 Navy Seal officers are black, or 1 percent; among the enlisted men—only 2 percent of the Seals were black, Green Berets had only 5.4 percent that were black, the Marines, both officers and enlisted combined to total 1 percent black, and out of the Air Force's 166 Pararescue jumpers, only one was black (0.6 percent).[1] The results of a 1925 US Army War College Study revealed that "blacks are mentally inferior, by nature subservient, and cowards in the face of danger. They are therefore unfit for combat." During this time the US Military believed that Black Americans lacked the courage, intelligence, and skill to succeed in combat. Is this true? If so, what does it mean? How did

---

[1] Brook, Tom Vandon. "Pentagon's Elite Forces Lack Diversity." USA Today, August 6, 2015. https://www.usatoday.com/story/news/nation/2015/08/05/diversity-seals-green-berets/31122851/.

those perspectives impact me? Why would my mom send me such an article, what was she trying to tell me? Looking back, I know she was trying to protect me. Protect me from failing in such a grand undertaking. Just after 9/11, being a personnel officer, she was quite aware of how many forces were being called out to war. Maybe by trying to protect me, she in fact was protecting herself. No mother, not even a second-generation active-duty officer who believed in the military, would willingly want to send her child to war.

Have you ever wanted to do something big, but been told that you can't for whatever reason? You are too small, not smart enough, you have past failures, the color of your skin? The story contained in these pages, details some of the lessons I learned having the opportunity to attend the hardest school in the Army, the Special Forces Combat Diver Qualification Course, affectionately known as CDQC or simply "dive school". My opportunity was much different and quite frankly much easier than most of the African Americans that went before me. In the end everyone's experience is different. That means there are different obstacles and challenges. Many reading this book will have different experiences than me. Though different, the difficulties are still valid. What matters is what we do with our opportunities. My training to become a Green Beret grew my mindset to not settle with that accomplishment, but to have greater goals and want to join the lineage of becoming an elite combat diver. The tribulations and triumphs experienced throughout my training taught me more about myself than any other event in life and simultaneously grew my faith in God.

Over 70 percent of the earth's surface is covered in water. Every day we use water to clean, drink, work, and play. We live in a world where water is all around us and the failure to have dominion over it is killing us. According to the World Health Organization 372,000 people die from drowning each year, that is forty people every hour of every day. We must learn to master the water. We must learn to swim.

The purpose of this book is not an autobiography about me. It's to encourage you! I share my story, not to offer a strategy, but to offer a glimpse into the posture of my heart as I was exposed to various trials. My experience is as a Green Beret who happens to be black, but it's a story for anyone who has experienced the weight of being told they could not accomplish something, anyone who has been reminded that they did not belong. It is a story to remind you that God is faithful and what He calls you to do, He will enable you to do. It is written to motivate you toward growth and change. What have you been told that you cannot accomplish, that you can seek God to bring you through, not for your own good, but for the Kingdom's sake? It is my hope that after reading my story, you too will be equipped with hope and courage to conquer fear and doubt and make your mark.

> "Water is magnetic and I began to feel its pull."

1

BORN OR MADE

For you equipped me with strength for the battle; you made those who rise against me sink under me.
—2 Samuel 22:40

In his book, *Contested Waters*, Jeff Wiltse tells the story of a Little League baseball team, in 1951, that decided to celebrate its championship win at the local municipal pool in Youngstown, Ohio. When the players and coaches arrived at the pool with their parents and siblings, not everyone could get in. One baseball player, Al Bright, was denied entry because he was black and had to sit outside the fence while everyone else played in the pool. A few of the parents pleaded with the lifeguards to allow Al admittance. Eventually they "compromised"—Al could access the pool for a few minutes if everyone else got out of the pool, but Al had to sit in a rubber raft. As the lifeguard pushed Al in the raft around the pool, he kept reminding him, "Whatever you do, don't touch the water."

Just thirty years later, at five years old, I was first introduced to the pool. My parents, both active military and stationed at Lakenheath AFB in England at the time, carried very busy schedules. They often provided me with various recreational activities to keep me engaged. This time it was swim class. I don't remember a large part of the *class*. I don't remember being taught much beyond how to float. They definitely did not teach any strokes or any type of swimming form. I can't even remember how long the class was in total. What sticks out to me is that they made us jump in and swim a certain distance every time.

I didn't know much at five, but I did know there had to be a better way. Every single stroke took all my energy and required every ounce of my strength to keep myself above water. There were so many things that I was doing wrong, there were so many ways that my technique could have been improved to be more efficient, allowing me to save more energy. There were so many ways to improve my body position and rotation to give me more power and result in swimming at faster speeds. Every time I lifted my head out of the water to breathe, my hips sank and I turned entirely vertical, bringing my forward momentum to a halt. I would have to wait twenty-five years to learn a few tricks to allow me to swim faster and easier. Later I would learn that increasing the downward angle of my stroke would push my hips up to the surface, decrease drag, and conserve energy. Instead of frantically kicking my legs with my chest facing the bottom of the pool, I could swim more efficiently if I swam on my side, switching sides with each stroke—propelling my body through the water.

Finally, it was time for the exam. To pass the course and earn my certificate, I had to swim the length of the pool, down, and back. This was extremely frightening to me. We had never even practiced swimming a single length of the pool. I remember not wanting to be first, so I shuffled myself to the middle of the line, and as my time again came near, I reshuffled myself to the very back of the line. Time had run out. No more shuffling, no ability to hide as I was the only black kid in the group and easily stood out. It was now time to go! Everyone else was done, with gigantic grins and basking in the glory of their new accomplishment.

I am still standing there terrified. So many thoughts were racing through my head. What happens if I can't make it? Why isn't there a lifeguard? Who will save me? I also felt an extreme amount of pressure. I didn't want to be the only kid not to finish. I was fully conscious of the difference in my skin color in 1981. We were less than twenty-five years from the height of the racial violence and discrimination that took place at municipal pools and only eighteen years after the desegregation of schools. Race relations in society had barely moved forward. As the only black kid there, I didn't want to be the only kid that couldn't make the swim.

Time was not on my side, as I had drawn quite a bit of attention from the instructor, the kids, and the parents whose eyes were all on me, sitting in silence waiting to see if I would in fact jump in. This is exactly what I didn't want. But with my knees shaking, I took a deep breath and jumped as far as I could toward the other side of the pool. It felt like I would never stop sinking toward the bottom. Eyes open, I swam back up to the surface and toward the distant wall. Under the surface, I could swim like a fish, but that wasn't the assignment. Even still, I used this to my advantage to gain as much distance as possible. As soon as I surfaced, it felt like my head was as heavy as a fifteen pound bowling ball. Each time I lifted my head up to both exhale and inhale, my hips would sink creating drag, causing me to swallow the highly chlorinated water and both choke and panic. I could not get to the other side fast enough.

I had no heroes in this sport. None that resembled me or otherwise. I had not seen any movies or read any books to assist in building my vision to learn how to swim. I didn't have regular access to a pool at this point in my life, so water was unfamiliar and dangerous. Swimming was literally just an activity that my parents put me in to keep me busy, it was likely cheaper than daycare, and it came with an added bonus—guaranteed exhaustion at the time of pick up. Little did I know that this experience was a must in my life and was preparing me for something great many years later. At five years old, I did not know why, but I did know that quitting was not an option!

The struggle to reach the far side of the pool continued. I took one last breath, put my head under the water, kicked and pulled the water with my hands as hard as I could until—finally my hand touched the wall. I latched onto the wall for dear life. I thought there would be nothing that could pry my little black fingers away from that rail. As I hyperventilated and tried desperately to catch my breath, there stood the instructor, telling me to let go of the wall and continue to swim. I wanted to stop, I wanted to be saved from this torture.

We are wired to value immediate rewards in comparison to future ones. This explains why we are so prone to easily quit in the middle of any hardship, surrendering to instant gratification in exchange for any potential future success.

I couldn't see where my parents were, but I knew they were there. They put no pressure on me to make this swim; they probably couldn't have cared less, but that was not the thought in my mind. I could not quit in front of my parents. I would not quit in front of this crowd. I remember the British kids laughing at me the first day I got in the pool because my hair "didn't get wet." I could not give them more to laugh at and I would not give them the satisfaction in saying black people couldn't swim.

With one deep breath, I submerged my head while still holding onto the wall with one hand, curled both legs up like a spring and pushed away from the wall as hard as I could. I swam as far as I could subsurface, but eventually I had to come up for air. I was hoping I would be further, but I wasn't even a quarter away to the other side. As I initiated my version of the freestyle stroke, I quickly began to fatigue. Evaluating the energy I had left in my tank, I was convinced that reaching the other side was physically impossible. But I didn't have much choice. I was in the middle of the pool. Too far again to turn back and too far from either side to make a pit stop and grab onto the gunnel. I was scared. I wasn't afraid of drowning in that pool. I was afraid of embarrassing myself, my parents, and my race by being the only one that could not complete the swim.

It would have been easy to quit at this moment. I don't think anyone would have blamed me. But now that I was in the middle of the pool, quitting was not an option. I had to make it to the other side. And that is what I did. When I reached the other side, hopping out of the pool with excitement—no one was watching other than the instructor and my parents. Everyone had already moved on, the pressure that I felt was self-imposed. I hadn't really learned to swim; I had learned not to drown.

Only a few years later, at seven years old, I had another frightening meeting with water. Enrolled as a student at Rocky Bayou Christian School in Niceville, Florida, I attended their summer camp. Both of my military parents worked long hours as part of the nature of the job—so they were not home during the day. So, it was either camp or a babysitter. Camp please!

The camps were fun though. Looking back at it, many of the activities, though legal, weren't entirely safe. One activity we did twice a week was to drive to a few different bridges, park on the side of the road, stand on the rail and jump in. It had to have been at least a ten-foot leap. I don't recall ever seeing anyone go and check to make sure the water was deep enough or to make sure no one had tossed an old refrigerator at the bottom of the small creek. Nothing was safe back then. This was the era of three-wheelers, driving while piled up in the back of a truck bed, and staying outside all day until the streetlights came on. Seat belt laws wouldn't even come into effect in Florida until three years later in 1986.

The dark murky water would immediately dye your clothes coffee brown. It was extremely fun, but terrifying. Not only was the height of the drop scary, maybe it was my imagination, but I am almost positive that I saw the boogie man in that creek water on a few occasions, and maybe even a few random body parts. My goal for those days was to not touch the bottom to avoid having to confront whatever mystery lurked there.

One of my favorite activities of camp was to go to Mr. Mosley's house as he lived on a lake. There were lots of activities. You could fish, swim, or raft.

It was a hot day, a day that dawned much like a thousand other summer days under the Florida sun. That day, I decided to raft. There were at least ten of us on that small raft. We had no idea what we were doing, yet we all tried to take command of the oars as if we were professionals. With four oars in the hands of random kids, the raft spun slowly in circles as it drifted toward the far bank of the lake. Mr. Mosley didn't give us much in part of instructions, but he did warn us not to go to the far side of the lake as there were a host of water moccasins over there. Now in the middle of the lake we began using the raft as a diving platform. Diving off the platform pushed the raft further toward the water moccasins' habitat, but we continued playing unaware. Once we realized the danger we had put ourselves in, unable to properly paddle away from the far side, we jumped off, abandoning the raft.

I was the sole camper left on the raft. I was terrified; it was a long swim and I was really uncomfortable attempting to swim that distance. The longer I thought about it, the longer the swim became. Now everyone had left, and I wouldn't have anyone to turn to for help. In my mind, I had two options: drown or get bitten by a couple of venomous water moccasins. I chose to try my luck at making the swim.

I swam as fast and far as I could. I swam fast trying to catch up with the group, but that was to no avail. I experienced a host of emotions from joy that I had swam further than ever, to agony, realizing that I still had a long way to go. My legs began to signal that I was going to cramp. Not only was every muscle in my body fatigued, but my brain was exhausted trying to fight through the panic. I couldn't fight anymore. I had accomplished so much, but I was still going to drown. I was too tired to even call out for help, as I attempted to open my mouth to call out, it filled with lake water and my head sank beneath the lake's surface. My legs followed suit and I sank to the bottom of the lake. Through all the splashing and struggle, I had no idea that I had made it far enough to simply stand up and walk to the shore. In my fit of panic, I thought I was going to drown in that murky water, but something else happened that day—I became a little bit more comfortable in the water.

My relationship with the water was further developed the following summer, on the beach in Hawaii. It was the first time our family had taken a big vacation. Although I loved playing in the sand on the beach, the ocean water was majestic. My parents tried to impress on me the brutal power of the water, but its beauty continued to beckon me, and I could not stay out of the beautiful crystal-clear water off the Hawaiian shores.

Back in Florida, my access to pools increased. During my childhood, I was fascinated with swimming subsurface. I loved games that involved swimming underwater, especially "sharks and minnows". As an only child, I didn't always have people around to play those games with, so I often had to keep myself entertained. I loved sinking down to touch the ceramic tiles at the bottom of the pool. All I needed was a coin and I could spend hours repetitively throwing the coin in the deepest part of the pool and diving to retrieve it.

The weightless feeling of swimming underwater gave me a fixation of trying to control my breathing and heart rate as a kid. There were parts of swimming that were more appealing than simply exercise. I would hide in obscure places, then wait for extended periods of time trying not to run out of air, trying to breathe so shallow that there was no rise and fall of my chest, so my breathing couldn't be heard, revealing my hiding place. Teaching myself to be comfortable in the water, I often bypassed safety. Timing my breath holds, I would spend hours with my head subsurface in the bathtub, always trying to break my own records. At the time, I had no idea why mastering breathing and being comfortable doing so was important, but time would tell that story.

After three years of living in Florida, my parents received Permanent Change of Station (PCS) orders to Hampton, Virginia. Moving a lot, I became an expert at making friends fast. Brandon, who lived on the same street, quickly became my best friend at the time. We did everything together. We played on the same soccer team. He introduced me to the James Bond movie series. Moving from Florida, I introduced him to the Miami Vice TV show series. We would dress up in suits with tank tops and ride our bikes around the neighborhood, with replica guns strapped to us in leather shoulder holsters that his dad gave him.

Brandon's dad was a Webelos den leader. Brandon begged me to join, so we could spend even more time together. I joined, but it was always a strange time for me. We met once a week on Wednesdays and I was introduced to so many things that were foreign to me. My dad never came, not because he was a bad father or something like that, but simply because that was not part of our culture and interest. After my first year, we aged out of Webelos and transitioned to the Boy Scouts as we hit middle school. Scouting gave me my first experience of leadership opportunities and exposed me to many activities that I would never do as a part of my family, such as camping. To this day, I have never gone camping with my dad and for no explainable reason. It's just something *we* didn't do.

Scouting further developed my relationship with the water. Over the summers at Scout Camp, I earned the Swimming and Lifesaving Merit Badges. Neither merit badges were easy *As*. There was a cost of admission. For the first time I learned the four fundamental swim strokes and had to demonstrate my ability to perform each stroke while swimming for 400 meters without pausing. I also learned to float. This is when I understood that I was built differently and what was a relaxing five-minute float requirement for most, was five minutes of mayhem for me. I don't know the physiological explanation of it, but due to my body composition, I simply struggled to float. Pursuing these badges also exposed me to various rescue techniques that would prove advantageous years later in dive school.

I made it all the way to the rank of Star, two ranks away from becoming an Eagle Scout before quitting just before entering high school. I was a three-sport athlete and I told myself that I had no time. Truth is I was tired of being made fun of for being a Boy Scout. I had no idea what I was giving up then and I still regret not finishing.

Water is magnetic and I began to feel its pull. I never took private swim lessons nor was I on a swim team, we didn't have a pool, my parents didn't own a boat. My access to pools and the open water was limited, but any chance I had to get in the water, I did. I began to love being in the water. These experiences began to shape my relationship with water. Still having a high regard for the fierceness of the water, I began to feel comfortable in the water.

Many land animals are born with the instinctive ability to swim, but being in the water is not normal for humans. Born incapable of breathing underwater and without the instinctive ability, humans must be taught to swim. Similarly, are you born with the unique skills needed to become a Special Forces Combat Diver? If not, can it be taught? It's an important question that deserves a thoughtful response. Some argue that you must be born with the ability and a person cannot be made to have these qualities. I agree with former Delta Force Sergeant Major Kyle Lamb, "that no one is born into this, we are made into this as we go through the training process."[2] Sports psychologist Graham Jones believes that elite performers in both sports and business are not born, but made.[3] I would argue a little bit of both. You must be born with the innate ability somewhere inside you, but that is not enough. It takes training and discipline to bring that ability out and to be made into an elite Special Forces Combat Diver.

It's through our various experiences and training that we can be shaped into having what is demanded to serve in special operations. When the bullets start flying, it isn't normal to be in the middle of a battlefield,

---

[2] Lamb, Kyle. "Backed by Science, Powered by You." *Backed By Science, Powered By You-*, evenpulse.com/lesson/special-operators-born-or-made. Accessed 24 Mar. 2023.

[3] Jones, Graham, "How the best of the best get better and better." *HBR's 10 Must Reads on Mental Toughness.* Boston, Massachusetts: Harvard Business Review Press, 2018.

surrounded by gunfire and remain perfectly calm. It certainly isn't normal to run towards the sounds of gunfire to engage the enemy at the risk of one's own life, but thank God, as George Orwell reminds us, there are that select few that stand ready to do violence on behalf of those that are sleeping peacefully in their beds at night.

Operators are made, not innately gifted with some sort of magical talent. You can grow in development. Even Jesus grew in development. In Luke 2:52, the Bible describes four areas of development: wisdom (intellect), stature (physical), in favor with God (spiritual), in favor with man (social). Over the next few pages, I will share with you the mindset that I learned through training to be a combat diver.

Application:

What were you not born with the talent to do, but feel in your heart called to do? You must believe that the talent can be developed. Albert Einstein didn't start talking until he was four, didn't start reading until he was seven, and was thought to have a mental handicap. Yet his name is synonymous with intelligence. Take the risk to pursue what you were called to do and don't give up until you make your mark.

"The Team SGT responded, 'Black people can't swim,' and slammed the door. This dismissal deflated me."

2

THE COVETED GREEN BERET

When I entered the Army, I had no idea what Special Forces was, let alone a Green Beret, but it wasn't long after joining the Army that I knew I wanted to earn the Green Beret. Less than two years after I entered the Army, I was now over two-thirds of the way through the Special Forces Qualification Course (Q-Course) and it was time to personally test my theory of whether Special Operators were born or made.

It was bad luck to buy your Green Beret before completion of the course, but in my assurance (ok, arrogance) and eager anticipation of donning the coveted Green Beret, I purchased my Green Beret right after passing Phase IV, Robin Sage and just prior to entering the last phase, Phase V, SERE School. During the few weeks between phases, I began shaping it. This task was a ritual that every Green Beret cherished. One would take that floppy beret that you bought at military clothing and sales, place it on your head, tie the knot off to fit the size of your head, grab a brand-new set of disposable razors and begin shaving the beret down as far as possible without shaving a hole in it. This took hours to get it just how you wanted it. Finally, when you thought it was close, you submerged the beret in hot water and then placed it on your head. The last step was to mold and form the beret to your head. This process, although seemingly simple, was significant, as it has been said the Green Beret says more about you than you could ever say about yourself, so you wanted to look good.

After graduation, my mentor who was a seasoned Green Beret, SGM Conrad Fernandez, RIP, told me congratulations, hugged me, and told me just how proud he was of me. But that celebration was short-lived. His next sentence was, "That was the easy part, now the real work begins." What? Are you kidding me? I just busted my butt and completed the hardest feat of my life up until that point and that's it? A congratulations lasting only about two seconds and now it's back to business? Celebrating a successful completion of training for too long will lead to complacency. Back to business indeed!

After celebrating graduation from the Special Forces Qualification Course (Q-Course) and receiving my Green Beret, the party ended. I immediately had to report to Alpha Company, 3rd Battalion, 7th Special Forces Group. I had been waiting for this day for over a year. Likely it was closer to two, as I had recycled Phase III, the MOS portion of the 18C (18 Charlie

- Special Forces Engineer Sergeant) Course for failing my demolition exam by a point.

My arrival to the unit was a simple case of bad timing. I arrived at the unit as one of only a handful of black SF (Special Forces) soldiers. I had my Green Beret in hand, Long Tab on my shoulder, lean and in peak physical condition. Having spent over a year of my life training to become a barrel-chested freedom fighter, in my own mind, I was ready for war! I was ready to prove what I had become. I was ready to become battle tested, only to make my grand entrance to a ghost town. As I nervously, but anxiously opened the door to Alpha Company, 3rd Battalion, 7th Special Forces Group, I walked into an eerie dark hall with no visible activity. Standing in the doorway, which we called the fatal funnel, I stood confused. To the left was the door to the B-Team. I didn't know much at this point in my career, but I knew enough to know that I wanted nothing to do with the B-Team. So, I walked past the open door of the B-Team, continuing down the dark hall, hoping to see a familiar face as a few of my friends had graduated the class ahead of me and had already reported to the unit. I was unsuccessful. Where was everyone at? Who would in-process me? Finding no answers, I was left with no choice, but to turn around and report to the B-Team. I had missed all the A-Teams and my chance to deploy stateside for Pre-Mission Training (PMT) by just two short days and I now tragically found myself assigned to the B-Team until their return.

It was the end of September and I found out that the unit would deploy to Afghanistan in January. I had three months to prepare. Prepare how? My entire unit was already gone in a training phase. Each day I reported to the B-Team to do clerical work and answer phones, trying not to lose motivation. When I was in the Q course, I was selected by my achievements and leadership to go to the E-6 board. I was more than prepared for it. The morning I arrived, I walked in and the first question by one of the board members was, "How long have you been in the Army?" I told him, around three years. Coming in with a college degree, I was given the rank of E-4. In the Army, rank from E-2 to E-6 can be achieved by working hard, being squared away, maxing out your military and civilian education, maxing your PT test, and not getting into trouble. If you wanted to be promoted, the ball was in your court, the only things stopping you at times were the time-in-grade and time-in-service requirements. Yet, in the Army there is a waiver for everything.

Not this time! Even though I fulfilled the time in grade requirements, I was given a waiver for the time-in-service requirement by the cadre because I was thought to be squared away. The cadre didn't care. He ripped the written waiver up in front of my face and kicked me out of the board. I was devastated, the cadre members that recommended me were devastated, but it was what it was. I was told not to worry about it. I could go to the E-6 Board as soon as I graduated and got to my team. Well, that time was now. It just so happened the board was coming up, while I was sitting around *guarding* the phones every day. I boldly asked the sergeant major if I could attend and he quickly shot me down. He said, "Hell no, you just got here. You can go once you get assigned to your team."

During this time, all I could think about was what team I was going to be on. This was during a time when Special Forces was trying to build up to a 4th Battalion. So, it just so happened I would have been the 3rd 18C on any team I joined. I had to stay motivated. I looked for motivation and inspiration wherever I could find it. There was a young captain also assigned to the B-Team that didn't treat me *as* terrible as everyone else. I tended to have more conversations with him than anyone else and began to watch how he carried himself. One habit he had was going to the pool to swim laps during lunch. Intrigued by his daily ritual of dragging his cool diver gear out of the team room, wanting to see exactly what he actually did in the pool, I made the mistake of asking if I could go with him. He didn't have time to spend teaching me anything, so luckily, I could only watch. I became deceived as this experienced combat diver, made every technique look easy.

Before the A-Team returned, the SGM told me that I was going to be assigned to the mountain team. The mountain team? I didn't yet know what team I wanted to be a part of, but I knew it was in no way the mountain team. Making a habit of climbing mountains in freezing cold temperatures didn't sound like a fun time to me. Being young and fresh out of the Q Course, I had an eager desire to go to the best team and be surrounded by the best operators. Quickly, I learned the team that had the best reputation in the company for being the toughest and fittest was ODA 775, the dive team. To this day, no other team in Alpha Company would admit that fact, but when you talked to people independently, no one that wasn't already on the dive team wanted to go through the torture of dive school.

Going through the training to become a Green Beret changed my mindset. It made me stronger. As I obtained goals, it gave me bigger goals. I now wanted to go through the most difficult training offered and volunteer for things that no one else wanted to. Ultimately, I wanted to be the best of the best. That narrowed my choices down to only two options—joining a HALO or SCUBA team. Every team already had their quota of two engineer sergeants (18Cs) each. The HALO team had their third 18 Charlie assigned to it just a few days before I graduated the Q Course and reported for duty. My desire to never want to experience a shallow water blackout was about to be over. Here I was contemplating expressing my desire to go to the dive team to the SGM to experience this self-inflicted torture.

Just a week after the SGM told me I was going to be assigned to the mountain team and it felt like I hadn't slept since. I didn't want to go to the mountain team. I was no longer satisfied with reaching my goal of graduating from the Q Course. If I was going to spend my time as a Green Beret, I had to be the best.

I put my big boy pants on and knocked on SGM Wright's door. "What do you want?" As my voice squeaked, I spoke, "Uh… SGM , can I talk to you for a minute?" His response, "What is it?" I continued, "Well, SGM, last week you told me that I was going to be assigned to the mountain team. I was thinking that every team is full of Charlies, so any team I go to, I will be the third Charlie. That being the case, can I go to the dive team instead?" The SGM looked both furious and confused as to who this kid was standing in the fatal funnel challenging his decision.

Having already been around this curmudgeon for a week, I fully expected this reaction to my request. With the puzzled look still on his face, he asked me if I knew what it required? I was prepared for this question, and I had already done plenty of research to best understand what I was getting myself into. "Roger, Sergeant Major, I do and I am prepared to go through the training." I also knew that there were three more

Charlies that were already assigned to the company from my Q course class that decided to take leave prior to reporting. It was my rookie mistake that made me the single soldier to report straight to the company without taking any leave, but at least I *should* be able to get first dibs on the team I go to.

SGM was still angry with me for asking him to change his decision. He looked at me, laughed, and while shaking his head no, replied, "What the hell? I will send you to 775." But he reminded me that not many people pass dive school and that I would only get two chances to pass dive school before they kicked me off of the dive team, and back to the B-Team I would go. That didn't scare me, and I didn't change my answer.

"Ok, get out of my office and go see the Team Sergeant of 775 and I better not hear you quit." "Roger, SGM—thank you!" The twenty-foot walk from the B-Team to the door of the ODA 775 team room felt like a twelve-mile ruck march. I had overcome one hurdle, but now I had to talk to the people that were going to make the decision. This was an advantage in Special Forces. The teams had self-autonomy to make their own personnel decisions to make sure the teams gelled and people were compatible. It was never uncommon for someone to mess up one evening and come back the next day to find their stuff in the hallway and the passcode to the cipher lock changed.

Now it was my turn to find out my fate with the team. I knocked on the door and took a step back, waiting anxiously and not knowing what to expect, what to say, or who to say it to. The door opened. It was Tim C., a new medic on the team, who had not yet gone to dive school. As I nervously began to explain what I was doing there, he interrupted and said, "You need to talk to the Team Sergeant." He shut the door and there I stood waiting to talk to the Team Sergeant.

Fifteen minutes later, the Team SGT opened the door. "What are you selling?" I responded, "I am not selling anything MSG, I am here because I want to join team 775." He replied, "Join our team? Our team's full." "I know, MSG, but as you know we are building up to a 4th Battalion and as a part of that, I will be third Charlie on any team that I go to. I heard that 775 is the best and I want to be a part of the best team in the company."

He responded, "Black people can't swim," and slammed the door. This dismissal deflated me. My life experiences up to this point in my life had protected me from such nonsensical thinking. Special Forces guys had a special way of finding your differences (in this case it wasn't hard). Once they found them, they would poke at them to exploit your weakness. There was no Diversity Equity and Inclusion (DEI) representative on a team. Anything was game. You better not show even a moment of weakness or that something bothered you or it would get even worse. It was mostly a part of weird machismo bonding, but not entirely. Special Forces soldiers equate to approximately one percent of the Army and combat divers make up only one percent of that one percent. It didn't matter what color your skin, dive school was difficult for anyone to pass.

Application:

People have no power over you unless you give them consent. The choice is yours. What power will you choose to grant people? Will you chase your dreams or believe what people say you can't do?

“At the beginning of the nineteenth century, apparently 80 percent of the black population knew how to swim, versus 20 percent of white Americans.”

3

BLACK PEOPLE CAN'T SWIM

A man is not learned until he can read,
write, and swim.
—Plato

I couldn't let it show, but those words did bother me. I was well aware of my limits and had taken over a year to earn the Green Beret. I had spent many days cold and wet coming face to face with them. But I despised being reminded of them, particularly by people that didn't know me. Having earned the Green Beret, in 2005 when I was preparing to go to dive school, I looked around my unit for motivation. Seventh Special Group had over 1,400 soldiers at the time. This number included Special Forces qualified soldiers and support operations soldiers. Out of the 1,400 soldiers, there were zero black soldiers that wore the Combat Diver Badge. I wasn't afraid of the water, but I wasn't swim team material either. Maybe it was true, could black people really not swim?

Today there is an alarming amount of black people that do not know how to swim. The USA Swimming

Foundation reported in 2023 that 64 percent of African American children have little to no ability to swim. Why is this number so high? Years of racially segregated pools may be the blame. But there is a culture among some black people that think it unimportant to learn to swim. For some, fear of the water has been passed down generationally, others have the mindset of swimming being a white sport, and not for black people. Whatever the reason, it is important for blacks to learn to swim, for one simple reason—learning how not to drown.

It hasn't always been this way. Although many black Americans today have little affinity for swimming, there is a rich history of swimming dating back to Africa before slavery. At the start of the seventeenth century, European explorers boasted of the swimming ability of West Africans. Pieter de Marees, speaking of the freestyle swimming of Africans from the Gold Coast, said they "swim very fast, generally easily outdoing people of our nation."[4] Swimming was embedded into the life and culture of the West Africans. Their coastal communities gave them access to oceans, lakes, and rivers, and the ability to experience the water from a young age. Much like today, swimming created a way for Africans to relax and cool off from the sweltering African heat together

---

[4] Dawson, Kevin. "Enslaved Swimmers and Divers in the Atlantic World." The Journal of American History. Vol. 92. No.4, 2006. 1331.

as a community. Beyond community, the skill of swimming offered jobs such as fishing and diving. Gold Coast Africans were especially sought out to be employed as pearl divers. Marees also noted:

> They are very fast swimmers and can keep themselves underwater for a long time. They can dive amazingly far, no less deep, and can see underwater. Because they are so good at swimming and diving, they are specially kept for that purpose in many Countries and employed in this capacity where there is a need for them, such as the Island of St. Margaret in the West Indies, where Pearls are found and brought up from the bottom by Divers.[5]

The slave trade brought not only the West Africans to the Americas, but their abilities to swim as well. Francis Frederic, a former slave, implies that most slaves knew how to swim in his statement, "Unlike most slaves, I never learned to swim."[6] Lynn Sherr in her book, *Swim: Why We Love the Water,* offers support for the robust history of swimming among slaves stating, "Before the Civil War, more blacks than

---

[5] Pieter de Marees, *Description and Historical Account of the Gold Kingdom of Guinea (1602)*, trans. Albert Van Dantzig and Adam Jones (Oxford, 1987), 186, quoted in Kevin Dawson, "Swimming, Surfing and Underwater Diving in Early Modern Atlantic Africa and the African Diaspora.'" Chapter in *Navigating African Maritime History*, edited by Carina E. Ray and Jeremy Rich, 81-116. Research in Maritime History. Liverpool University Press, 2009.
[6] Dawson, 1345.

whites could swim." She continued, "There are many stories of shipwrecks in which black slaves rescued their owners." It's necessary to grapple with the parts of our nation's past that are difficult, but it's also necessary to positively move beyond the difficult parts of our nation's history toward the future.

Many people are unaware of how the Underground Railroad got its name. The story is told that in 1831, Tice Davids, a Kentucky slave, escaped slavery by swimming across the Ohio River. While chasing him in a boat, Davids's owner lost sight of him. Believing Davids had drowned, he remarked that he must have taken an "underground railroad," and the phrase has been in use ever since.[7]

Mikael Rosen in his book, *Open Water: The History and Technique of Swimming,* states that, "At the beginning of the nineteenth century, apparently 80 percent of the black population knew how to swim, versus 20 percent of white Americans. Many slave plantations were located close to lakes and rivers, and a quick bath in nature with some soap was the only chance for slaves to freshen up after a day of sweaty and dirty work."[8] In the early days of slavery, many slaves began

---

[7] Pitts, Lee. "Black Splash: The History of African American Swimmers." 2007. 1. 12 April 2024. https://www.yumpu.com/en/document/read/7600375/black-splash-page-1-international-swimming-hall-of-fame

[8] Rosen, Mikael. *Open Water: The History and Technique of Swimming.* Chronicle Books: San Francisco, CA.

learning to swim between the ages of four and six.[9] Recognizing the swimming abilities and lung capacity of their slaves, some slave owners put their slaves to work as pearl divers and lifeguards aboard boats. But after seeing that swimming provided an organized system of escape, owners began to prohibit their slaves from swimming. Soon slave owners began to take more drastic measures to keep their slaves from escaping by swimming. They began to instill a fear of the water. They dunked their disobedient slaves in water and told stories of dangerous creatures living in the water. This new fear of the water coupled with preventing slave children from learning to swim began to remove the West African swimming tradition from the African American culture.

Due to slavery and the fear of the water, black people had limited access to water. At the turn of the twentieth century, America started to build pools, despite the African American culture's decline in the use of swimming for recreation and safety. The first public pools were built in inner-city disadvantaged neighborhoods. These pools were racially inclusive and served as bath houses for low-income and working-class individuals. Initially, American swimming was divided along gender and class lines, but after World War I in the 1920s, men and women were allowed to swim together, and pools became family

[9] Dawson 1344.

gathering spaces that fostered communal socialization. Everything changed after World War I when racial discrimination became accepted and institutionalized throughout the country. Carter G. Woodson described the environment of soldiers after World War I, "Negro soldiers clamoring for equality and justice were beaten, shot down, and lynched to terrorize the whole Black Population."[10]

Americans had more leisure to swim and engage in other recreational activities since they worked less and earned more. The increasing freedom for men and women to interact in pools sparked fears about interracial mingling. To prevent black men and white women from mingling in this location, governmental officials implemented racial segregation. "As a result, blacks were banned from entering public baths and beaches and 'white only' signs went up next to public pools."[11] While the North employed violence and intimidation to keep black people out, the South utilized Jim Crow legislation to maintain pool segregation, and pools became violent battlegrounds for racial strife rather than recreational areas.

This is difficult for me to fathom. As I write this in 2024, I think about swimming with my children. I

---

[10] Delmont, Matthew. *Half American – The Epic Story of African Americans Fighting in World War II at Home and Abroad.* New York, NY. 2022.
[11] Rosen, 55.

am reminded of perfect summer weather, where people of all races, genders, and social classes commune safely together at pools. I can recall countless cannon balls, lots of splashing, and uncountable games of Marco Polo.

Prior to this, racial desegregation resulted in widespread desertion of public pools. White Americans evacuated cities and moved to the suburbs, where they built backyard and private pools. Wiltse writes, "Between 1950 and 1970, millions of Americans chose to stop swimming at municipal pools."[12] Shortly after President Lyndon B. Johnson signed the Civil Rights Act, which prohibited segregation based on race, color, religion, sex, or national origin. As cities stopped funding public pools due to lack of use, pools began to close. Many of the pools that didn't close fell into disrepair, lacking funds to keep up with the maintenance. The opening of private pools allowed controlled access to both pools and swim lessons.

One of my favorite stories of heroism is of Fred Rogers. In 1969, though segregation was no longer the law, Black Americans were still prevented from swimming alongside white people. Fred Rogers knew that pools continued to refuse entry to blacks and that racial tensions were rising; just a year earlier, Martin Luther King, Jr., had been assassinated. Yet, in this atmosphere, Fred Rogers asked Francois Clemmons, a

[12] Wiltse, Jeff. *Contested Waters A Social History of Swimming Pools in America.* University of North Carolina Press, 2010.

black police officer to join him on his television show *Mister Rogers' Neighborhood*. Mr. Rogers performed a simple but meaningful act inviting Officer Clemmons to cool his feet off in a kiddie pool. Officer Clemmons initially declined the invitation because he didn't have a towel, but Mr. Rogers said Officer Clemmons could share his.

In less than three minutes of episode 1065, Fred Rogers and Officer Clemmons showed that a black man and a white man could peacefully share the water by taking off their shoes and socks and swishing their feet together in the kiddie pool. They exposed the bigotry of denying black citizens access to pools, or other places in society. The long history of discrimination in pools and elsewhere could not be erased by this one episode, but Mr. Rogers's brave act was a huge step toward black and white people swimming together.

Growing up as a military brat in the '70s into the early '80s, I had the privilege of always being near a military base where I had access to both indoor and outdoor pools. Living in a suburban neighborhood, my family didn't join local swim clubs, but I was always welcome to tag along with friends whose family did have access. In my college years, I worked as a lifeguard over the summers. I remember being shuffled from the prestigious suburban pools to more urban pools. I didn't mind because I relished the time to help young boys and girls that looked like me fall in love with the water, much like I had.

Today, this problem continues as there are an estimated 10 million residential pools and only 300,000 public pools. It is no longer as much about race, but with the closing of many public pools, access to pools is limited to those who can afford it. The racial gap in swimming that persists among blacks today is not due to inability, but due to lack of access. Within the last several years, there have been notable black swimmers that have climbed the ranks in US Olympic swimming.

After nearly drowning, Cullen Jones's parents put him in swim lessons, he learned to swim at only five years old, and eventually became the first black swimmer to both hold a world record and win an Olympic gold medal. He is a four-time Olympic medalist (two gold, two silver) and a two-time gold medalist at the World Championships. Sabir Muhammad while at Stanford University was the first African American swimmer to set an American record (100 butterfly) in 1997. Also from Stanford, Simone Manuel was the first African American to an individual Olympic gold medal at the 2016 Olympic games. As the 2024 Olympic Games approach, Anthony Nesty, who first made history in 1988 by becoming the first black male swimmer to win an Olympic gold medal will make history once again, becoming the first black US Olympic head swimming coach as he leads the men's swim team this summer in Paris.

Swimming is more than a sport. It is an essential life skill that must not be taken for granted. Learning this essential life skill will not only decrease the number of drownings, but just like in the seventeenth century, it can open a host of not only leisure activities, but employment opportunities as well.

The history of blacks having limited access to pools was not the end of my story. The story takes a sharp turn. Even though blacks were once excluded from combat roles and restricted from attending dive courses in the military, I would one day soon have the opportunity to attend dive school.

"Every action and reaction carried with it life or death consequences."

4

COMBAT

Humans are more important than hardware.
—First SOF Truth

After a bunch of begging, pleading, and lobbying, I found myself on ODA (Operational Detachment Alpha) 775, the prestigious dive team, as the third 18C. This was my chance to accomplish something the world by default told me was impossible. But after joining the team, I was constantly reminded that I was not a combat diver and I was not "really" a member of the team until I passed dive school. I needed to prove the theory wrong. It wasn't out of pride, but out of necessity. I needed to know, was there a reason that I felt drawn to the dangers of the water? Finding out if I could swim would have to wait as it was time to prepare for deployment to Afghanistan.

Arriving in the theater, the "friendly" reminders continued. Being a Christian and having a former soft-skill MOS (Military Occupation Specialty) of Chaplain Assistant made it worse. To them, my grit and poise under fire had never been tested and once again I was not a combat diver. I needed to prove myself to them. As the deployment progressed, I believe the team began to trust us four new guys on the team, however the ridicule never slacked.

I was "selected" to be a part of the Advanced Echelon (ADVON) team that arrived in Afghanistan ahead of the rest of the unit to begin coordinating to receive the main element. On January 4, 2006, I boarded a plane on familiar turf only to get off eighteen hours later in an unfamiliar land. From the security of being at home to the insecurity of war—literally overnight. I was both excited and frightened at the same time. After receiving a likely million dollars' worth of training to become a Green Beret, I was ready to go to war. But I missed the training with the team.

Being the new guy on the team and having missed all the pre-deployment training, it was probably a good thing that I was voluntold to become the team's representative on loan to the battalion as Alpha company's area specialist team (AST)—to serve as a point of contact for all actions between the ODAs on the ground and special operations task force (SOTF) leadership. But I wasn't happy about this. I wanted into the fight, but for now, seeing the battlefield would have to wait.

Being the company AST was no small assignment. The requirement was for a senior Special Forces noncommissioned officer (NCO), but somehow as a lowly E-5 that had less than three years total in the

Army, and only a few months in the group, I found myself thrust into this responsibility to track missions and advise the SOTF commander on all of the teams in Alpha Company.

I was likely voluntold for this position for two reasons. One, it required me to deploy a month earlier than everyone else as a part of the advanced party. As I deployed just after the new year, the senior members of the team wanted to stay home as long as they could to spend more time with their family. Two, having spent months in pre-mission training, these guys were ready for combat! This was our battalion's first deployment to Afghanistan. There were some that had deployed as a part of other units, but only a select few had seen combat in this theater as a part of 7th Special Forces Group.

My duties reporting to the SOTF commander required me to work a twelve-hour shift seven days a week. I spent the rest of my time working out, eating, sleeping, or watching terrible copies of American TV shows on pirated Afghan DVDs. This occupied my time and kept me from going stir crazy and from missing home too much. In this position, it was my job to be the answer man. If teams needed (or wanted) it, whatever *it* was—I was expected to both find it and get it manifested ASAP on a flight out to the teams at the firebases. I was certain this assignment was going to make or break my reputation within the group and

I could not fail. I am generally a quiet guy with little to no personality. This wasn't going to work. To pull this off I needed to transform into a bit of a car salesman and a politician. Having to quickly build rapport, find a need and fill it.

I was promised my time as an AST would be short and that someone from my team would replace me within a few weeks. Many weeks went by with this promise being broken. As my time as an AST continued to be extended, on February 13, 2006, while working in the OPCEN, the 9-Line MEDEVAC (Medical Evacuation) request came across the radio from Alpha Company's other dive team ODA 785. Waiting for the 9-Lines of the request seemed like an eternity. And then it came, Line 3—we were informed that the team had suffered three KIA (Killed in Action). While on vehicle patrol in the Uruzgan Province, an improvised explosive device detonated hitting their vehicle and killing combat diver SFC Chad Gonsalves, along with three others, SSG Edwin DazaChacon, SSG Clint Newman, and Sgt. Alberto Montrond. Only a month into theater and 3rd Battalion, 7th Special Forces Group, had just taken their first losses in Afghanistan.

This was Chad's first combat deployment in Special Forces. News reports quote his mother recalling that Chad had wanted to be a Green Beret since he was in the sixth grade. "He was born for this." When I thought of what a combat diver should be like, it was

Chad. Chad probably didn't even know who I was, but I looked up to him. He was hard as nails, and I always saw him around the company grinding and doing hard things.

Our unit had lost brothers and I was stuck pulling twelve-hour shifts in the OPCEN. I had to get to my team and get into the battle!

When I finally flew into firebase Chamkani to join my team, I was beyond ready. Chamkani was in the eastern part of Afghanistan in the Paktia Province, a few kilometers from Pakistan. Before joining the Army, I lived right outside Washington, DC, on 9/11 when American Airlines flight 77 was hijacked and crashed into the Pentagon. I lived with a small group of students from Uzbekistan. They came to the US to attend Bible college and they had a heart for Afghanistan. They often told stories of sneaking into Afghanistan as missionaries and having underground church services at the risk of getting caught and having their heads cut off. For nearly six months, every Sunday, they invited a small group of people to join them in praying for Afghanistan—that they could go there freely. I always thought about going with them, but with working full-time, living check to check, and starting grad school, it was never an option. But now I was in Afghanistan.

No time to settle in, I wanted to be outside of the wire. One of the benefits of being in Special Forces was that we dictated our own missions (at least at this point in the war). We collected our intelligence and created our own targets. Our small ODA honed in on the enemy following the F3EAD cycle (Find, Fix, Finish, Exploit, Analyze, and Disseminate). As Special Forces soldiers, we were good at what we did. We used speed, surprise, and violence of action to bring the fight to the enemy. We operated in the night, striking when our enemies least expected. We had developed a High Value Target (HVT) and now it was time to go and get him. I was amped and I felt invincible. I had put in a lot of work to be ready for this very moment. It was time to go to war for my country and I believed I was called to engage in this fight. I was so amped that it was noticeable. Alex, one of the Senior 18 Charlies, asked, "What is wrong with you?" I remarked back, "Wrong with me? Nothing is wrong with me. I am ready to go." Alex replied, "You obviously have never been in a fire fight. Once the bullets start zinging past your head, you will wish you were back here." Had he lost his mind? I was built for this, and I had been waiting to serve in this war for several years now. But Alex was right, once I heard the crack of gunfire and the first bullet whistled past my ear I was dialed in and completely aware that this wasn't a game. Every action and reaction carried with it life or death consequences.

The focus here is not to describe combat as a Green Beret, there are many solid books that do a great job at that. The legitimate question of my first of many combat deployments was: what was the lesson to be taught here? I learned to put into practice everything I was taught in the Q Course, but I also learned that there wasn't a SOP (Standard Operating Procedures) for most solutions. I had to think outside of the box. Throughout the Q Course, I heard repeatedly, "If you're not cheating, you're not trying." That wasn't a call to behave unethically. It meant to push the limits. From day one of Special Forces training, we were being untrained as much as we were being trained. To be experts in unconventional warfare, we needed to remove all the conventional military training that we had previously been indoctrinated in. It wasn't enough to simply do what you were told, utilize muscle memory to operate weapons and equipment without having to think, and respond to the same old battle drills. Terrorism changes as rapidly as technology. Battle drills for the type of war we were facing didn't always exist. We had to anticipate the enemy and be agile. The lessons I learned in Afghanistan would serve me beyond the military, they would serve me the rest of my life. I became a professional problem solver.

When soldiers leave the military, they often struggle initially. Surrounded by people that have been taught not to think for themselves, people that need to consult the SOP. Leaving a group of high-speed problem solvers for this new environment makes this transition difficult. The world needs thinkers, leaders, and creatives—people that can find solutions within themselves. War as a Green Beret wasn't about displaying bravado. It was about winning hearts and minds, which necessitates thoughtfulness.

Application:

"Write the vision; make it plain on tablets, so he may run who reads it. For still the vision awaits its appointed time; it hastens to the end—it will not lie. If it seems slow, wait for it; it will surely come; it will not delay."
—Habakkuk 2:2-3

Are you willing to do something that scares you? Do you have a vision for your future? Have you made it plain and written it down? You have to define your dream before you chase it. Having a vision statement for your life will provide a clear destination while providing a road map to fulfill your calling. Create a vision board where you display your vision and goals. It will allow you to protect your vision and keep it at the front of your mind, helping you to avoid distractions.

"Was I strong enough?

Was I tough enough?

Was I up for the challenge?

Was it too difficult?

Was this a part of God's will

for my life?"

5

MAYBE THEY ARE RIGHT

There were four of us that deployed to Afghanistan as a part of ODA 775 that had not gone to dive school. We redeployed back to Fort Bragg, NC, in September 2006. Despite nine months at war with ODA 775 and coming home with a Bronze Star, I knew I wasn't really on the team because I was reminded daily during the deployment that I had not passed CDQC, and I didn't have my Combat Diver's Badge (Bubble). I began to think maybe they were right. Maybe black people can't swim. What was the purpose of even going to dive school, only to fail, embarrass myself, and eventually get kicked off the team anyway?

I needed to know. Was I strong enough? Was I tough enough? Was I up for the challenge? Was it too difficult? Was this a part of God's will for my life? So, I had to train. During the deployment when we weren't outside the wire, we were training. We trained hard, most often pulling two-a-day workouts. We lived at about 8,000 ft above sea level and either ruck marched or ran the observation posts loop up to 10,000+ ft each morning. In the afternoons, we lifted weights and finished with even more cardio. Eight months of this routine intertwined with combat missions brought me home in peak physical and mental condition. But I still had doubts. How was this mental and physical conditioning that I did on land going to help me in the water at dive school? I would soon find out as we had only a few weeks to prepare for the pre-scuba course conducted by the same "teammates" that reminded us that we were not a part of the team.

I caught up with family briefly, but I had no time, I had to get into the pool! I joined the YMCA in Fayetteville, NC, right outside of Fort Bragg. They were used to joes coming in there doing dangerous breath hold exercises and swimming laps for hours in full uniform and fins. They had also grown so tired of telling us to stop with the breath hold exercises that they gave up and let us train at our own risk.

Once we arrived, it was another busy time with redeployment and change of command leading straight into pre-scuba. I am positive I would have much rather attended a pre-scuba somewhere else other than with my team. Having the senior members on my team as instructors was horrifying. It is as if they couldn't wait for the golden opportunity to torture us each day. To them they had gone to the last hard dive school class and Key West wasn't the same anymore. In their minds, we were not going to get the same torture they received when they went through, so they had to give it to us before we went. It didn't matter who you were, the water is the most dangerous training ground because on the shore it looks so peaceful. But with its beauty—it lures one to draw near, forgetting its power, and without any notice, you can experience both its energy and its rage. A combat diver must contend with the tides, depth of the water, currents, and dangerous marine life.

One day, having a very full workday, I rushed to Raleigh for an event. But I had to get my training in, so I took my dive booties and fins to a gym in Raleigh. When I walked alongside the pool, it was full of people of all ages swimming. I always made a habit to put eyes on the lifeguard to try to get a sense of how they were going to react to me jumping into the pool in full uniform and fins. Train as you fight! This time though, I decided to only swim in shorts and fins, so as to blend in as best as I could. Except there was no lifeguard in the stand or on the deck. I put my dive booties and fins on and slid into the pool and began swimming my laps. The goal was to get two miles in practicing the combat swimmer stroke, the technique that I would need to have mastered if I wanted to pass the two-mile ocean swim and the seven-minute sixteen-pound-weight-belt swim in Key West, Florida.

While on my second lap, I rotated my head out of the water to breathe and saw a silhouette of a person resembling a lifeguard. Continuing to fin, I noticed this person pacing alongside me. I took five more minutes of this before abruptly stopping in the middle of the pool to ask what she was doing. She was either offended or surprised by my question—maybe even both. Putting her hands on her hips, she huffed and said, "I am making sure you are ok." Making sure I was ok? What in the world? How could I not be ok? Swimming laps in a pool five feet deep. If I got tired I could just swim to the other side, stop and take a break. Better yet, I could simply stand up and walk to the other side.

I was left dumbfounded. Where was she with the pool full of swimmers before I arrived? Why did she choose to focus only on me as if I needed saving? There are a lot of reasons why this middle-aged Caucasian lifeguard would have this reaction. Only three percent of the membership of USA Swimming are black.[13] Black children are three times more likely to drown than white children.[14] Although there have been a host of talented swimmers representing the US, it is still a rare sight to see black swimmers.

---

[13] Whitten, Phillip. "African American Swimmers Why the Disparity." *USA Swimming Home,* 1 Feb. 2017, www.usaswimming.org/news/2017/02/01/african-american-swimmers-why-the-disparity.

[14] Lawrence, A. (n.d.). *Giving kids a lifeline.* Black Children are three times more likely to drown than -08.23.10 – SI Vault. https://web.archive.org/web/2012111415044/http://sportsillustrated.cnn.com/vault/article/magazine/MAG1173390/4/index.htm.

At some point, you begin to question. You question God's vision. You question yourself. *Are you strong enough? Are you tough enough? It's too difficult. Maybe they are right, maybe you can't swim!* But God never calls a person to do something he cannot do.

What about the doubters, the people that truly believed that black people can't swim? What about the people that looked me in the eyes and told me that black people can't swim? What about them! I am thankful for them. That's motivating. There was no way I could allow people to tell me I couldn't do something. The more I heard that it was impossible for black people to swim (joking or not), the more I wanted to prove everyone wrong, to include myself. Now I get to prove them wrong by doing something they said was impossible.

I remember first being introduced to the Tank Tread exercise in pre-scuba. For many, being poolside reduces stress, increases feelings of happiness, even leads to awe and tranquility, but for us, it was about inviting suffering and fear. Standing on the pool deck staring at the sixteen-pound weight belt and the two twin eighty tanks, we listened to the pre-scuba instructor discuss the event. All I had were questions. You want me to do what? Jock up in all that gear and tread water for how long? Five minutes, that's the length of the Tank Tread exercise. Wearing twin eighty-liter tanks, a sixteen-pound weight belt, and other equipment totaling 100 pounds of gear, keeping both your head and hands out of the water, the task is to tread water for five minutes. Grab onto the gunnel even once, you fail!

Being negative buoyant, I was already at a disadvantage. This event was a dog fight for me. I had to master my technique, but at about two and half minutes in, technique goes out the window. The goal then became to remind myself to take long strokes with my legs, focus on my breathing to keep my heart rate down, and try not to panic! Breathing is a matter of life and death and maintaining focus is easier said than done when you watch one of your friends go unconscious and sink to the bottom of the pool wearing 100 pounds of gear.

Combat divers affectionately called passing out in the water "meeting the wizard." To this day, I am probably one of the few combat divers to have never met the wizard and I still have a healthy fear of meeting him. Although the pre-scuba cadre are very good at peeling the gear off and getting people up to the surface immediately, the negative image of seeing one of your friends on the edge of the pool being revived and getting a minute or so under an oxygen mask becomes seared into your brain forever. That day, while continuing to tread water, it would be Captain David G. I watched being pulled to the surface, revived on the deck before being thrown back in the pool, and asked if he wanted to quit or continue to train. At that very moment, I felt as if I were the author of Psalm 69.

Save me, O God,
for the waters have come up to my neck.
2 *I sink in the miry depths,*
where there is no foothold.
I have come into the deep waters;
the floods engulf me.
3 *I am worn out calling for help;*
my throat is parched.
My eyes fail,
looking for my God.
—Psalm 69:1-3

Application:

This world will often give you reasons why you *can't* become who you were meant to become, but it is imperative to ignore the counsel of your critics. We all have critics in our lives, they are the people who don't understand our dreams. Refuse to believe that there is any possibility that the critics are right. Critics will always inform you that it's impossible for you to do something incredible. Don't let anyone's opinions cause you to reconsider your vision. What we believe will determine our ability. It's not going to be easy, in fact, it will be hard, but that is why it's valuable.

Two-time Olympic Champion Eliud Kipchoge is said to be the greatest male marathoner of all time. In a quest to do the unthinkable and break the two-hour barrier in the marathon, he failed with a time of 2:00:25, missing the mark by a single second per mile. This was an incredible achievement to even get this close. Instead of praise, this attempt incited the voice of critics throughout the web. Kipchoge did not listen to the critics and two years later in a Nike time trial, he broke the barrier, crossing the line in 1:59:40 and proving that "no human is limited." To put that achievement in perspective for non-runners, that is a pace of 4:34.5 per mile for 26.2 miles. I can't even run one mile that fast. Kipchoge proved to himself and to the world that no human is limited and any human being has the power to go beyond their thoughts.

"Completing this exercise
required more than the
power of discipline
and positive thinking.
It required faith."

6

DROWNPROOF

Fear not, for I am with you; be not dismayed,
for I am your God, I will strengthen you, I will help you,
I will uphold you with my righteous right hand. Behold,
all who are incensed against you shall be
as nothing and shall perish.
—Isaiah 41:10-11

Much is revealed about us through our preparation. My kids are athletes (runners). As I coach them, I often point out that their races aren't won in the actual moments of the race. They are won or lost well before the event. The result often comes down to how they did or did not prepare.

For every military school that I have attended thus far in my career, I prepared for it with the mindset of taking myself to the deepest, darkest depths of pain that I could, so that anything asked of my body and mind during the school itself was seemingly easy. Pre-scuba was no different. Except this time, I was not the one taking myself to the deep dark places, it was my teammates.

I spent much of my military career in awe. I couldn't believe I was getting paid to do this. As I stood with my toes just behind the edge of the pool, hands behind my back, both my hands and feet bound, staring at the twelve-foot depth marker, I was certain that this wasn't a time that I would be in awe. I was about to be introduced to the event known as Drownproofing.

Drownproofing was one of the most horrifying experiences of dive school. It is exactly what it sounds like, a survival technique originally developed by swimming coach Fred Lanoue to survive drowning and adapted by the military to make it a torturous survival technique. What was supposed to be easy and meant to offer most people rest, was extremely difficult and felt impossible for me. Floating is simply physics and I couldn't float! There is positive buoyancy, neutral buoyancy (ideal), and there is me—negative buoyant! I am not sure why, some say that black people's bones have a difference in mineral density, others say it is body fat distribution. I am completely unsure why, all I know is that I can take a very deep breath, fully inflating my lungs with air, and sink straight to the bottom of the pool and take a nap. Let me tell you, this is not the preferred technique.

This pass or fail event had six evolutions. It began with your dive buddy securing both your wrists and ankles with two Velcro straps while you stood at the edge of the pool dreading the audible command to "enter the water". How could I not think of the time back at the lake where I almost drowned? I was still the same person who was a weak swimmer and couldn't float. Only now I was hogtied with my hands and feet bound. There was an art to this exercise though—too tight and the straps could easily be kicked loose from the power of one dolphin kick. Too loose and it leaves you depending on your muscles to keep your hands and feet together, wasting energy that you would definitely need later in the event. Either one of these were causes for the cadre to immediately stop the event and issue an automatic failure and a plane ticket home.

At the command to enter the water, you take one last deep breath and simultaneously jump in the water, with hands and feet bound, and begin to bob. To get to the bottom of the pool, you must begin exhaling as soon as your feet break the surface. It feels like it takes hours, but in reality it is only a few seconds until your feet touch the bottom. The first bob is the easiest because you have momentum working with you. This part of the exercise is actually where being negative buoyant helped me and I was able to reach the bottom of the pool faster than most. Once your feet touch, you can't rush to the surface. Instead, you allow the weight of your whole body to come to the bottom with your feet, compress into a tight spring, and push off the bottom to return to the surface. This requires caution. Push off too hard and you risk breaking the restraints, which is seen as a form of panic.

Continue to exhale on your way up, to get rid of all of the carbon dioxide buildup in your lungs, making room for a bigger mouthful of fresh oxygen. Once your lips break the surface, you open your mouth as wide as possible and gasp for air before heading back down.

This evolution of the exercise lasts five minutes. Your hands and feet must stay bound while you continue this portion of the exercise. At this point, two things are important: to stay relaxed, and to keep your heart rate down. Merriam-Webster's dictionary defines panic as a sudden unreasoning terror often accompanied by mass flight. The minute you panic you are done for.

Eventually, I got to where I could enter a near meditative state. I could only think about the present. I couldn't think about the last three minutes or so that I completed because if I broke my focus, those minutes would no longer matter. I also couldn't think of the next twelve to fifteen minutes of the test, because that too would break my focus and send me to a state of panic. Ignoring the past and the future, I could only think about the immediate moment.

The next command given is to float for two minutes. For most, this is a relaxing two minutes, for me, I could have used a fancy tech suit to improve my buoyancy keeping my hips closer to the surface. While in the fetal position, I lift my head quickly to the surface to fill my lungs with air quickly. With my head back in the water, I execute a few slight kicks returning my body to the surface and *try* to relax. Holding my breath as long as I can, I must continue to kick to stay near the surface. Just before needing my next breath, I exhale underwater. My experience is much different than most. I spend two minutes rhythmically kicking hard or at the bottom of the pool. Remaining in this position, the next command requires using a dolphin kick to complete a 100-yard swim around the perimeter of the pool. As I travel around the pool, my heart rate raises, and my brain analyzes the data of the situation, it is tempted to be alarmed. As my brain begins to crave air, it deceives me into thinking I am in a survival situation. Our brains always seek to solve survival-related problems. It is not the brain's fault. Proper brain function requires oxygen and due to the hyperventilation, my brain is not receiving its necessary amount of oxygen. In this instance I must override the message that my brain is sending and remind myself it is not real. I had to control my emotions.

Our brains can be trained to perform better. They can be trained to think faster, process information more quickly, and perform executive functions better. Choosing to persevere through challenges builds the mental strength and resilience needed to not only handle adversity, but to thrive in it. Through the successful completion of these exercises, we become less inhibited by stress and develop stress resiliency.

The only way to stay afloat now is to swim faster, continuing to move forward to avoid sinking to the bottom—but this again raises the heart rate. My heart was racing, vibrating against my rib cage. My heart emitted the sound of a rapid firing bass drum, and it echoed loudly. After traveling, I have five recovery bobs to try to get my heart rate down and prepare for the mask retrieval.

Returning to the deep end of the pool from the swim, I am required to execute a front and back flip. Immediately after completing the flips, the instructor drops a dive mask. At this point, your heart feels like it is going to explode. Completing this exercise required more than the power of discipline and positive thinking. It required faith. I had to rely on my faith through this uncomfortable experience. I had to retrieve the mask, secure it in my teeth, and complete five more bobs. After all of the previous effort, if I fail to complete the bobs, accidentally break the restraints, drop the mask, or touch the sides of the pool, I fail.

Application:

Drownproofing is mostly mental. I had to learn to handle the pressure and navigate around it. My body is not built for it and it constantly sends signals to my mind that I cannot complete it. It is imperative to turn this part of my brain off because the body follows the mind. When your brain tells you that you have had enough, but you haven't reached your physical threshold, push the wall further away. What is something that your body tells your mind that you cannot complete? What have you done to train through it?

> “This vision began to shape what I believed. With this vision, the die was cast. I felt a need to change the message that black people can’t swim.”

7

WHAT DO YOU WANT TO BE?

A month after 9/11, I entered the Army's Delayed Entry Program. This was a program where you committed to join the military later and participated in monthly training while you awaited your enlistment date. March 2002 had finally come. I was locked in a motel room not far from the MEPS station in Baltimore, MD. It was my last night of "freedom" before the bus came to take us to Army basic training the next morning. Unauthorized to leave and unable to sleep, I found myself surfing the channels. Tired of channel surfing, I settled on a random documentary about Army Survival Evasion Resistance and Escape (SERE) School. It was like watching a bad train wreck in slow motion, but being unable to turn away. I don't remember much, but I remember people being smacked around and put into tiny, dark places with bags over their heads. I couldn't believe this was legal. My parents both made a career out of the Air Force, I knew absolutely nothing about the Army. After watching the documentary, I knew one thing—I never wanted to go to that school! Shortly after the documentary, there was a commercial for the SEALS or some sort of Special Operations water training. And with that little clip of water training that made two things I knew about the Army—I knew there was no way I wanted an introduction to either of those schools.

God has a funny sense of humor. As a part of becoming a Green Beret, I had already completed SERE school and now I found myself in Key West, Florida, at Special Forces Underwater Operations School attending the Special Forces dive school. Dive school's training compound is remotely located at the far end of Fleming Key on the Naval Air Station Key West, a naval base just ninety miles off the coast of Cuba. It is not for the faint of heart or feeble mind. It is the most physically demanding course in the United States Army and is as demanding mentally as it is physically. Deceivingly calm, water is the most dangerous environment to train in. Success requires not just swimming, but a deep understanding of the ocean environment. In six weeks, the cadre of dive supervisor instructors would train us in dive physics, Navy dive tables, dangerous marine life, and medical training—to understand the effects of deep-water injuries on divers. We would train to open and closed-circuit dive. We would master the depths of the ocean, the tides, the currents, and the latest in innovative science and cutting-edge underwater technology and learn to use underwater operations tactics to infiltrate into denied enemy territory undetected. Using water as a clandestine way to defeat an enemy is not new. The story is told that Scyllias and his daughter Hydna, in 480 BC, armed with only knives and snorkels, swam underwater to cut the mooring lines of the Persian ships causing some to sink and others grave damage as they were tossed about by the wind and waves.

What do you want to be? This question was asked daily in dive school, before, during, and after most events. But the time to provide an answer to this question wasn't once I had arrived at dive school. I had to answer that question well before I arrived at the grueling six-week course. This question could only be answered with confidence as a result of my training. If the answer was to be a combat diver, then, it had to be seared into my mind and into my heart. There was no other acceptable answer. Failure was not an option. The answer to that question also had to be bigger than myself. It needed to be rooted in my faith, attached to the Supreme Being, a calling from God Himself.

Being told I couldn't do something was always a strong motivator for me to succeed at something. It wouldn't be enough to pass dive school though. Nor would my comfort in and enjoyment of the water be enough to keep me from quitting when it got hard. I needed more. I needed an internal flame to burn deep inside me.

Answering this question gave me that flame. More than that, it gave me a vision… it gave me a calling.

This vision began to shape what I believed. With this vision, the die was cast. I felt a need to change the message that black people can't swim. I felt I owed it to those that paved the way before me to be successful. Now I no longer had to question myself, with each stroke I took in the water, I had to believe that I was doing what I was supposed to be doing and I was in the space where I belonged. The goal no longer was just to pass dive school; I had to master the water and prove my abilities beyond a shadow of anyone's doubt. Attending dive school, something bigger than myself, something that I was not "supposed" to do, was an opportunity not to prove that I am superhuman (I already knew that I was not), but it was an opportunity for me to trust God.

MAKE EVERY EFFORT

We were to have our gear in perfect condition, lined up, and for inspection before we began PT at 0515 each morning. Even before the sun came up, the humid Key West air was oppressively dense. Breathing that air felt as if one had wrapped a wet sock around your face. Waiting in the dark, dreading the inevitable when the cadre would come out of nowhere sounding off with, *"Right face… double time… MARCH!"* The distance of the runs was always unknown. How fast do you run when you don't know how far you will be running? I despise long-distance running. As a former sprinter, anything longer than 200 meters is torture.

Not only do we not know the distance, but we also don't know the pace standard. To this day I don't know. I was told just don't fall behind the instructor with the ChemLight. The cadre were always fresh. As we ran, the cadre would follow behind in a vehicle and switch out often with fresh instructors that could keep us at the fast pace. Not long into the run, the formation would divide into ability groups. I could muster enough energy to stay in the first group, but it would break me off to do so, as they were running six-minute miles. The second group felt like seven-minute miles and the third group eight-minute miles. I had no problem fighting to stay in the first group, if it would have been of benefit—if we ran faster, we finished faster. Instead, I found myself having to run further for being in the fast group. Every half mile or so, we would stop to form a circle and commence to do the gamut of pushups, sit-ups, flutter kicks, squat thrusts, and whatever other masochist exercises they could conjure up, until the rest of the group caught up. Either way, I was wise enough to know I was being systematically punished for working hard. I also knew that the second group was well ahead of the ChemLight. So, my strategy became to run in the second group.

I wasn't safe there though. SFC Smith was a nut and for whatever reason didn't like me or wanted to make me better. Either way, he called my name more than my mother did when I was little and gave me a lot of "special attention." Not to mention SFC Smith was the most unassuming freak of a runner I would ever meet.

SFC Smith would show up at local marathons around Key West, win the run and, like Forrest Gump, not stop, run straight to his car and go home. Who was this mystery man? People began to inquire. The local papers wanted to talk to him, but he would refuse to talk to them time and time again. That is until—someone found out he was an instructor from the dive school, they called the dive school and the commander "highly encouraged" him to talk to the paper. He brought this same mentality to his leading the runs. I would try to get away from him, but he always found me. *"Brown, get up there!"* I would ignore him, "Get up there… get back in the first group or you will run extra." "I thought, yeah right." I was in the front of the second group and there were at least twenty people behind me. *Why are you even talking to me?* I made a flurry to get back in the first group, just to do a U-turn and go pick up the fall outs. *Are you kidding me?*

When we started back, I wasn't having it, I was staying in the second group. As a Green Beret, I had already been to SERE School and learned in situations like this they would just smoke us and break us off if we went 100 percent that early in the day. The run was the easy part of the day, we still had four hours of pool training and our ocean swims in the afternoon. I ignored his demands and I knew I had to be above the standard, but he didn't care. When we returned to the start point, after six miles, the cadre dismissed everyone to shower and breakfast. Everyone, except me that is. SFC Smith kept his promise and took me for an extra two miles. At least he ran with me (but he was a machine). He made an additional promise, if I didn't make it back in less than fourteen minutes, I was going to go for another two. I believed him and made sure he didn't have to prove it! This wasn't SERE School, I had to *make every effort.*

With the morning run behind us, we entered the pool. I now had a target on my back with SFC Smith. Every time I turned around, he was near me. When I couldn't see him, I heard him calling my name. We played many *games* in the pool. They were designed to wear you down before we began the testing events. It was now time for the Weight Belt Swim.

"Nut to butt, nut to butt!" "Line up, hurry up, get lined up, closer, tighter!" "Do it now!" All these things and more were being shouted at us while preparing to start our daily iteration of the seven-minute Weight Belt Swim. Like all the other exercises, this one sucked! The goal of the instructors was to create chaos by squeezing us all together on the gunnel at the start to induce panic. At the command *begin*, everyone fired off the gunnel at once, masks were ripped off faces, and fins were kicked off feet. Once again, grabbing the gunnel during the seven minutes or touching the bottom of the pool and you fail!

In contrast to the commotion on the gunnel, the water in the pool lay silent and perfectly still as if it were a giant predator, lying in wait to catch and devour its prey. The water was both unpredictable and unforgiving. Both the pool and the ocean were definitely in cahoots with the instructors' plan to weed out the fainthearted. Their plan was working. As we neared the end of week three, our original class of thirty-five had shrunk to about twenty. The class size dwindled every day. Between the fast runs, the stress inoculation in the pool, studying dive physics, and the open water navigation swims graded on accuracy and speed, people either quit or were beginning to not make the standard.

I always tried to get on one of the edges. I hated being in the middle. Today, I found myself right there in the middle of the pack and I knew what was in store for me. The only chance I had of making it through these seven minutes, was to spring off the wall with all my might and get out in front of the pack. I closed my eyes (couldn't see through all the splashing anyway), finned as hard as I could, and when I opened them, somehow, I was successful. There was only one person ahead of me—Joe Curreri. Joe was a beast. He only had two speeds. Fast and faster. He was a former Division

1 collegiate athlete like me. Unlike me, he was a D1 swimmer. I had been landlocked in my D1 experience as track and field sprinter. Joe was a former captain of the University of Southern California swim team and a scholastic All-American in high school. He was lean and still had his swimmer's body: long torso and upper limbs attached to broad shoulders with defined lats.

Despite not having much experience on an ODA while in dive school, Joe had a natural ability to lead, and people would always gravitate toward him. When Joe talked, people listened. He led by example and always did the right thing even when no one was looking. College degree in hand, in 2004, rather than become an officer, Joe opted to enlist in the 18X program. There he went straight from civilian life into the pipeline to become a Special Forces Operator.

Sadly, we lost SSG Joseph Curreri too soon. After graduation, he returned to his assigned unit, 2nd Battalion, 1st Special Forces Group. Only a few months after graduation, on his first deployment in support of the Global War on Terrorism, Operation Enduring Freedom, Philippines, he died in an accidental drowning incident on October 26, 2007. Soldiers like Joe are hard to come by, but the US Army has the world's greatest system for finding, recruiting, selecting, and training soldiers like him.

Joe was on Dive Team One. Being on the fastest dive team is a notable accomplishment and comes with bragging rights! Joe performed all the swimming events as if he were half machine, but watching him complete the Weight Belt Swim was particularly exceptional. He did it effortlessly. I wasn't proud that I was right behind him because that meant I was swimming too fast and my heart rate would soon be exploding out of my chest. Being out front and away from the traffic, I had to relax and get control of my breathing or I wouldn't survive this exercise. Although I hated this exercise, I trained hard for it. When training by myself, I trained with eighteen pounds instead of the required sixteen and I eventually got to the point where I could easily complete over seven minutes on my own. But I couldn't train for the traffic jams and congestion I would experience in dive school. I had a plan though. I had to swim with a fast tempo and maintain a high frequency of strokes to keep myself afloat. That meant I would swim way more laps than most people. I just could not stop swimming. As I got close to someone, I had to go subsurface and swim underneath them to end up in front of them and maintain my pace.

I couldn't escape the attention of the cadre. They didn't have to be next to me to recognize me, they could distinguish me from a mile away by my complexion. I knew going in that I would have to manage the stressors of dive school along with the additional weight of having more eyes on me and receiving *special attention.* Even subsurface the instructors extended their reach to me through the DRS (Diver Recall System), an underwater speaker system where I constantly heard my name. *Mr. Brown you are not doing the exercise. Mr. Brown what are you doing? Mr. Brown you are going too fast, you are going to pass out.* Luckily, I had mastered the ability to ignore my name being called as a kid.

We were about four minutes in and, even though I thought I was going to have a heart attack, my plan was working. While fighting my way through the exercise, I caught a glimpse of my good friend and roommate (back in Fayetteville, NC) getting out of the pool and walking to the cadre. This could only mean one thing, he had enough and was about to voluntarily withdraw from the course. I wanted to scream *no, don't do it*, but I could barely breathe as it was. Besides, I wasn't thinking about his feelings at that moment. I was thinking about mine. We had a deal! We were supposed to hold each other accountable. We were supposed to complete this together. How could he quit? The answer to that question didn't matter. Enough was enough, he had rung the bell. He could never come back.

Application:

Do you make every effort? Making every effort is a choice, not a talent. Having the road map that we discussed in Chapter Four isn't enough. You not only need to know what to do, but you must be willing to do the work. We have been taught for years to do the bare minimum at one task and then rush off to the next. Are you choosing to do more than the bare minimum to accomplish your vision? Are you willing to do whatever it takes to become the person people need you to be? You are capable of achieving your dreams, and when you do, you will discover that it was worth making every effort.

"My confidence in the water was a gift from God. He had been preparing me for this opportunity my entire life."

8

FEARLESS

But now thus says the Lord, he who created you, O Jacob, he who formed you, O Israel: "Fear not, for I have redeemed you; I have called you by name, you are mine. When you pass through the waters, I will be with you; and through the rivers, they shall not overwhelm you; when you walk through fire, you shall not be burned, and the flame shall not consume you.

—Isaiah 43:1-2

My senior year in college I worked as a security guard at a nursing home in Washington, DC. There was a man there named Mr. Pendarvas that was a resident there. He was well into his eighties, but looked no older than sixty. He was as sly as a fox. There were often groups that visited the facility. Mostly they came to volunteer, on rare occasions large groups of family members would come to visit their loved one. As these groups came to the facility, I would have to be on high alert. Mr. Pendarvas was slick and he always found a way to intermingle with the group and make his way outside and try to make a break for it! He was so good at getting outside, it was extremely stressful. Even knowing his plan, it was nearly impossible to avoid him making his way outside when the big groups gathered. He was a chameleon, he would somehow blend into any and all groups, wait for just the right moment, and slowly and methodically make his way out the door, slipping past the guard station.

One day, I heard one of the nurses tell Mr. Pendarvas as he meandered around the lobby in the crowd that the dogs were outside. Mr. Pendarvas replied, "Dem dogs outside?" "Yes, Mr. P, the dogs are outside." That was his kryptonite. When told this, he would immediately fold and go back to his room. I had seen pictures in books about riots, and how the police used dogs on black people during the '60s, but never had I seen anything like the fear that this man had of dogs. Seeing just how afraid he was of the thought of dogs being outside brought those pictures to life for me.

Culturally, blacks have a similar paralyzing fear of the water. A 2006 University of Memphis study cited fear as the number one reason that blacks did not learn to swim, and the absence of fear was the strongest predictor of swimming ability among the variables in the study.[15] This suggests that the fear that slave owners conditioned into blacks some time ago still lingers. Some believe anyone who is not afraid of the water is a fool. Yes, it is ferocious and has claimed its share of lives, but you don't have to fear it though you must respect it.

Blacks were not the only people afraid of the water. In the seventeenth century, Europeans believed in water monsters and the fear that stemmed from mysterious folklore creatures, such as the Loch Ness Monster, kept many from swimming in the ocean. While fear is a natural response, we do not need to be afraid. Mark Twain said, "Courage is resistance to fear, mastery of fear, not absence of fear."

Despite my lack of swimming ability and lessons, my access, and sporadic time spent as a youth in and around water making me comfortable in the water, I still had doubts circulating in my mind. Could I really swim or was my capacity limited to simply not drowning? My experiences in the Army taught me that as a black man, confidence in the water was rare. I often saw blacks excel in many training tasks until it came to water confidence. My confidence in the water

---

[15] Irwin, C., et Al. *Constraints Impacting Minority Swimming Participation Phase II.* University of Memphis, 2010. https://www.usaswimming.org/docs/default-source/parent/learn-to-swim/2010-constraints-impacting-minority-swimming-participation-phase-ii.pdf

was a gift from God. He had been preparing me for this opportunity my entire life.

While in pre-scuba, I memorized a Bible verse that gave me something to meditate on during breath holds. It allowed me to manage the stress, quiet my thoughts, and avoid succumbing to the panic and all the various emotions that it brings with it. Isaiah 43:1-2 brought me to places of great peace underwater. Wallace Nichols calls this calm and peaceful collaboration with water Blue Mind.[16]

I took the verses to heart. They reminded me that I was created and formed by God. I was known by name by God. The president of my local HOA didn't even know my name! I didn't have to be afraid of the water because I was redeemed. Meaning, I didn't have to fear death because if I were to die, I was secure in knowing that I would spend eternity in Heaven with God! I took comfort in knowing that God was not above me as a bystander observing me. No, this text says, He is with me! By placing my trust in him, I would not be overwhelmed, but instead experience peace.

Experiencing this peace wasn't magic, nor was it instantaneous. It took practice. I would certainly get plenty of time in the pool to practice. Through

---

[16] Nichols, Wallace, *Blue Mind The Surprising Science That Shows How Being Near, In, On, or Under Water Can Make You Happier, Healthier, More Connected, and Better at What You Do.* New York, NY: Little, Brown Company. 2014.

training, meditation, and prayer, we can reprogram how our behaviors and emotions respond to fear. We are not called to fear what following in the footsteps of Jesus may require of us. A life of following Christ releases fear.

Many have the knowledge of God's promises, but lack the courage only found in Him to live a life reflective of believing in His promises. Our faith in God's promises ought to be as Abraham's in Romans 4:20-21, "No unbelief made him waver concerning the promise of God, but he grew strong in his faith as he gave glory to God, fully convinced that God was able to do what he had promised." Abraham's faith was incredible, but I struggled to have the same response. As I doubted, it remained true that God was able to do what he had promised.

Application:

When I am afraid, I put my trust in you. In God, whose word I praise, in God I trust; I shall not be afraid. What can flesh do to me?

—Psalm 56:3-4

Ask yourself what are you afraid of? How do you handle the fear? Is your faith bigger than your fear? If you stop doing what scares you the moment fear sets in, it will go away, but so will any chance of accomplishing your definition of success.

I don't believe you can be completely fearless, as a healthy amount of fear serves as a reminder to take caution, but you can train yourself to be less fearful. Not succumbing to fear and running toward the things that frighten you is a skill that can be learned and taught. You can get better at it. Every single feeling of fear is an opportunity to practice pushing the wall of your limits a little bit further away. And with each repetition, you become a little bit more fearless. Do you practice not being afraid and pushing the wall further away?

"It's the lessons learned
and the humility gained
through striving to attain
something so big we know
we can't possibly do it
by ourselves and trusting
God in the process,
is when we succeed!"

9

FAILURE

Beloved, do not be surprised at the fiery trial when it comes upon you to test you, as though something strange were happening to you. But rejoice insofar as you share Christ's sufferings, that you may also rejoice and be glad when his glory is revealed. If you are insulted for the name of Christ, you are blessed, because the Spirit of glory[a] and of God rests upon you. But let none of you suffer as a murderer or a thief or an evildoer or as a meddler. Yet if anyone suffers as a Christian, let him not be ashamed, but let him glorify God in that name. For it is time for judgment to begin at the household of God; and if it begins with us, what will be the outcome for those who do not obey the gospel of God? And

"If the righteous is scarcely saved,
what will become of the ungodly and the sinner?"

Therefore let those who suffer according to God's will entrust their souls to a faithful Creator while doing good.

—1 Peter 4:12-19

Safety violations were normally punished with physical exercise, but this was the testing phase. There is no such thing as a bad day. Bad days are not allowed because mistakes equate to getting people killed. Mistakes, even in training, weren't allowed in Special Forces. After every training and real-world mission, we had a habit of highlighting both what we did poorly and what we did well. Under the microscope, mistakes were magnified and those that made them never heard the end of it. Mistakes equated to getting people killed. At this stage in my career, there were few things that made me nervous, but my body was infused with nervous energy. During an event that should have been an easy "go", the instructor said that I interrupted my breathing during my ascent of a pass/fail event. I say, the instructor said that I interrupted my breathing because I don't remember it that way, but it was what it was. I could not change anything. Having failed, I now had twenty-four hours to think about it before the retest. If I failed, I would be out of the course, so I rehearsed my sequence for several hours that night. There was nothing going to keep me from passing.

The next day couldn't arrive fast enough. I had passed all my dive physics exams up to this point and I was only two days from the One-Man Competency exam and getting out the dreaded pool phase. Before I could reach the One-Man Competency exam, I had to pass a very simple hands-on underwater test to ensure that I knew the sequence of fixing my equipment. At the beginning of the exercise, I was calm and my nerves were gone. I was adequately prepared and this test was nothing in comparison to combat. I entered the water with confidence and ran through each of the phases with ease. I had plenty of air in my tank to assure that I didn't interrupt my breathing. I ascended as trained and when I broke the service, I was notified immediately that I failed. I was in disbelief. I knew I didn't interrupt my breathing this time. I was right… but this time, I failed to kiss the manifold of my tanks before my slow ascent. I had crushed two and half weeks of this course and now I failed the simple stuff? Nobody fails this exercise twice. It was so rare that in my exit interview, the Sergeant Major of the school asked me if I failed it on purpose.

It's true, I was the only black guy there, received a lot of *special* attention, and was singled out more than anyone. I know what you are expecting to hear in this part of the story. I could blame any of those things for my failure, but I had no excuses. I could resort to a mentality and a belief that my failure was caused in some way by the color of my skin or to view the situation through a lens where I was a victim somehow, but through that lens, the truth becomes difficult to find. Failure is often simply failure. None of the instructors were acting as gatekeepers guarding the right from me to earn the right to wear the dive bubble by intentionally trying to make me fail. The truth is that although

I was given a lot of "extra" attention and there was a rare chance of passing because of the color of my skin, I was given a completely fair opportunity at earning my combat diver's badge. There was only one option, I had to learn from my failure and train so that it never happened again.

Failing dive school was devastating. I was already mad at myself and now I also had to listen to the naysayers. How could I go back to my team having failed? I knew I wouldn't have to look them in the eye and break the news. The Sergeant Major of dive school was a former ODA 775 team sergeant. So, I knew he had already made the call and told them the news. The flight home seemed like an eternity. Rehearsing scenarios of how the conversations were going to go. Hearing the ridicule. Worse yet, hearing, "We told you, black people can't swim!"

Failure often leaves us feeling broken. Have you ever gone through periods where you felt broken and alone? In this failure, I was tempted to feel sorry for myself and that God had forgotten me. On the other hand, it was through this trial, that I learned that only the promises of God were what could sustain me. Past black veterans overcame unimaginable adversity paving an opportunity for modern black soldiers like me. What would I do with my opportunity? I was not only failing myself, but everyone who had gone before me. My mother had two strikes against her in the Air

Force, she was a female and she was black. Watching her career, I was quite aware of the challenges of those that came before me and the privilege it was to attend this specialty school. Less than sixty years prior, it was not seen as acceptable. The Army's official position was once "that black servicemen were inferior as soldiers, officers, and human beings."[17] I knew intellectually that Romans 8:28 says God works all things together for my good, but I needed an encounter with God. I couldn't yield to the temptations to believe I was nothing, I had to stand fast to God's call for my life. I had to learn to trust God instead of myself.

When we look at elite operators, we are not privy to see the failures and the effort, the blood, sweat, and tears. Their success looks like it was gained effortlessly, but this is an illusion. We have to redefine success. There are many that will set goals to become combat divers and fail. This does not mean they are failures. Failure can be transformed into victory. It's the lessons learned and the humility gained through striving to attain something so big we know we can't possibly do it by ourselves and trusting God in the process, is when we succeed!

Failure is nearly inevitable in every part of life. The lesson was on how to react to failure. Does one

---

[17] Delmont, Matthew, *Half American – the Story of African Americans Fighting in World War II at Home and Abroad. New York.* New York: Viking, 2022.

simply give up and move on? I failed; it must not be for me. The greatest rewards are found in prevailing through failure. Prevailing through failure builds the muscle memory to be able to perform under pressure. Billie Jean King, regarded as one of the greatest tennis players of all time, once stated, "Pressure is a privilege. It only comes to those who earn it." Special operations soldiers have a dire need to perform under difficult circumstances. It is not something they should fear or attempt to avoid. They not only volunteered for the privilege, but have earned the right to be entrusted with the opportunity to lead both themselves and others to fight for our freedom.

In our failure we often feel alone and isolated. Jesus suffered more than we could ever imagine. Sweating blood, in great distress, Jesus fell on the ground, and said, "My soul is very sorrowful even to death" (Mark 14:34). If that were the end of the story, we would all be doomed. But we learn a lot from his response as he turns to the Father and prays, "Abba, Father, all things are possible for you, yet not what I will, but what you will" (v.36). He teaches us two things here. We can and ought to turn to God as a first response to our distress. It is ok to ask God to remove our suffering and change our circumstances. He longs to bless us. We must surrender our will and exchange it for the will of the Father. It was not God's will to remove the cup of His wrath from Jesus. Jesus accepted this decision and fought through the pain and agony to endure the cross. The Father said no to the son, the son trusted the father, and that led to the most meaningful event in history—the death, burial, and resurrection of Christ for our sins.

DRAW NEAR + TRUST + PRAY + SUBMIT

QUESTION

Are you struggling with fear and various trials in your life? You can pray just as Jesus did. Draw near to God, trust He can change your circumstances, pray, and submit your will to His. If we remain paralyzed by the fear of failing at something, we end up not achieving anything at all.

“Failure is one thing. Fear of failure is another. Never be afraid to fail. Doing so may leave you paralyzed—unable to even try.”

10

HUMILITY

"All these things my hand has made, and so all these things came to be," declares the LORD. "But this is the one whom I will look: he who is humble and contrite in spirit and trembles at my word."

—Isaiah 66:2

My failure's purpose was to humble me. The sovereign God who doesn't fail and conquered death began to use my failure to shape me. He used my trials for my good and for His glory. I learned that I was not defined by my failure. My identity rested in who Jesus was and what He had done. Who are you apart from your career? Don't be defined by what you do or don't achieve.

That wasn't my first time I'd failed in my life or career. It wasn't the first time I had been humbled. It wasn't the first time I had to recycle. I had already failed the Special Forces Assessment and Selection on my first try. Part of the twenty-one-day selection course was an event known as the Star Course. This is a ten-hour event that lasts for multiple days. During the event, you have ten hours to find four points. If you find all four points on your first day, you are done and you get to rest for the next two days while guys are repeating the course to find different points, only starting more tired than before. They say if you find your second point by the time the sun is coming up, you are good to go! I had found three of my points in the first five hours before the sun came up. Running the entire thing, I was crushing it and on my way to my final point. The points have point sitters for you to check in at and then give you your next grid coordinate. They were usually retired Green Berets that didn't mind camping out for a few days to be around the new recruits and make a few extra bucks. The points are marked with a Chemlight.

I was only 500-600 meters away and there was only one draw and hill standing in my way. As I was feeling good and super confident. I could see the Chemlight shining through, all I had to do was walk to it. I put away my compass and began running through the draw. The draw quickly began to swallow me whole. Before I knew it, I was twisted up and had resorted to crawling through the really dense terrain. When I escaped out of that Venus fly trap, I saw a faint neon light in the dark sky and began to run to it. I had wasted at least an hour, but it was still dark out. I probably should have taken my compass out for an azimuth check, but my arrogance led me right to a barn door with a random Chemlight hanging on it. It was 5ish in the morning, and I had arrived at a random farm with no one around. It didn't take a genius to tell me that I had made a grave mistake. It's ok though, I still had an abundance of time and all I had to do was find two intersecting roads and I could perform the crossroad intersection technique, locate myself on the map, and shoot a new azimuth to my point.

Without keeping pace count and chasing that dim light, I ran myself out right off of the course. Wherever I was standing, I did not have a point on the map. This was extremely dangerous. I was dressed in camouflage, had a rucksack full of military gear, and I was carrying a dummy rifle, and it was pitch black outside. A little over a year prior, two students were stopped by police during the exercise. The students thought they were roll players and during the exchange, the *real* police ended up shooting and killing one of the students. Not only did students have to watch out for cadre monitoring you with night vision, but in nearly every class at least one student would report back to the camp naked having been robbed at gunpoint by a local *hillbilly* who would take the gear from students to sell at the local military surplus store. For the next few hours, I ran up and down that area trying to get back on the course, but it was to no avail. I had failed and would be invited back to try again.

The first failure I chalked up to bad luck, but this time I knew it was different. What was I missing? It had to be for a reason. Was God trying to show me something? I am a doer that believes in getting things done. I believe in self-discipline, hard work, and persistence, but somewhere in this mindset it becomes easy to trust more on the work of your own hands rather than relinquishing your desires to God and trusting that even in failure He has a perfect plan for your life. Pride was my greatest enemy, but humility is my greatest friend.

I had asked God to help me, I pleaded with Him for help, I thought Psalm 37:4, said, "Delight yourself in the Lord and He will give you the desires of your heart." Was I not doing enough *delighting*? How could I continue to ask God for help after experiencing such failure? That is exactly what He wanted me to do.

The problem was not me, it was my method. I should have been praying, "Lord, if it's your will strengthen me, prepare me, and guide me." My mindset had begun to shift. If God had allowed this, it was for a reason. Yes, I wanted my bubble, but dive school began to be more than that. It was a chance for God to teach me more about Himself. It was a chance for me to learn more about myself. I didn't want to barely squeak by passing the course, leaving me unconfident in the water. Instead, it was important for me to have dominion over the water (Psalm 8:6).

God used my failure to imprint a clear message on my heart, "The heart of a man plans his way, but the Lord establishes his steps" (Proverbs 16:9). I didn't understand then, but I understand now, when I was elevating myself, I was robbing God of His glory. Before doing anything worthwhile, it was necessary for me to begin swallowing my pride. I needed to do nothing from rivalry or conceit, but in humility count others more significant than myself (Philippians 2:3).

My failure was not final. We love to root for the underdog, but society seems to love even more stories that end in the agony of defeat, but these failures couldn't define me. This chapter was over, but my story was not! While some saw it as a strength, my biggest weakness up until that point was the habit of depending solely on myself for every outcome. God was using this failure to humble and show me that self-realization and dependency on mental toughness, athletic ability, and my self-determination was utterly wrong. This failure could have broken me. In a big way it did, it broke me from the habit and mindset of believing the lie that all of my accomplishments were because of my personal hard work. This realization would change not only my career, but the way I lived my life. Failure is one thing. Fear of failure is another. Never be afraid to fail. Doing so may leave you paralyzed—unable to even try.

Although I was stuck in a world where pride is praised, my failure was the beginning of understanding my calling. Our world rewards pride, but God hates pride and arrogance (Proverbs 8:13). In my own head,

I was living the dream. I was a college graduate, I had the opportunity to compete collegiately, and I was a Green Beret with the privilege of serving my country. I had honed my skills to be an elite warrior who both craved and thrived in high-risk environments, but I wasn't humble. It's a difficult balance. To be exceptional at something, especially combat, takes a lot of confidence in oneself and in one's ability. I had confused this confidence with pride. I could always depend on myself. If I wanted to achieve something, I just worked really hard at it. That was my mindset, but where was God in that story? Where was God's glory? I didn't understand it then, but God had to bring me to the end of myself, seeing firsthand that on my best day, in my own strength I was yet nothing without God, but with God anything was possible. As He began to humble me, the more His eyes looked upon me (Isaiah 66:2). Having His gaze upon me meant that I also got to experience His grace and strong support (2 Chronicles 16:9).

God had to humble me. I was in a dangerous position. I was a prideful person who thought I was humble. I needed His help. I had grown unaffected and unaware of the pride in my life. I was trained to focus on myself. I made a habit of focusing on excellence and hard work. Anne Ottenbrite believes that "excellence eliminates doubt." In basic training, while waiting in the chow hall line, I would always pass by a poster. It had a headstone with RIP written on it and above it, a quote from Colonel James Nicholas Rowe, "Let no man's soul cry out, had I the proper training." That wasn't going to be me and there was no way I wanted to lose a teammate at the fault of my hands. There was no greater failure than to show up for war knowing you haven't done everything possible to be prepared.

It's ok to fail. Failure is normal. It's human. We are imperfect. We just can't wade in failure. I had to find courage to try again. I was promised one last chance.

Application:

Businesses today are in a leadership crisis as teams are finding themselves unable to handle failure. Organizations should be looking to hire people who have failed and prevailed not who have been blessed to make it through the first time. Hire those who didn't give up—those who have developed the ability to find a way or make one.

Through my failures I learned many lessons of humility and brokenness. Through that experience, I learned to make a habit of trusting God in each step forward. I haven't seen the last of my difficult days. Perseverance through suffering taught me valuable life lessons—to be humble, believe in someone greater than myself, and to fail isn't final. Our suffering is not in vain, through it all, we are being molded and brought to a greater point in our lives than we could even imagine. We were created for God's glory and to make much of Him. Our suffering now can't compare to the weight of glory to come.

TEARS

"Serving the Lord with all humility and tears..."
—Acts 20:19a

Years after this experience, one of the most beautiful things I have seen is an operator cry. To see a man, who has been so hardened by war and his experiences, find peace and joy again, and to be able to cry both tears of sadness and of joy, is mesmerizing.

The shortest verse in the Bible is John 11:35, "Jesus wept." Although it is a lowly two words, it is overly powerful. Jesus returns to the village and Mary meets Him, saying, "Lord, if you had been here my brother would not have died" (v.32). Jesus, seeing Mary and others weeping, was deeply moved. The word "wept" is *klaio* in the Greek, meaning that not only were tears shed, but Jesus' tears were a visible display of grief. A true man won't hide his tears, but we ought to learn from Jesus' experience with them. God cares about our tears, so much that He records them in His book and bottles each one of them (Psalm 56:8).

This crucible would shape my career. Not in a negative way, but it was all that I learned from the failure. This bit of turbulence in my journey made me stronger, more confident, committed to making every effort, and dependent on God.

We shouldn't be surprised by failure. The Bible says to expect trails. Our trials mold our character, refine us, and train our hearts away from trusting solely in ourselves. If allowed, our failure will do much needed deep soul work.

QUESTION

How do you respond when your dreams are suddenly shattered? What are your thought patterns? What actions do you take? When our dreams are shattered, we must trust in God's infinite wisdom.

"Instead of being 100 percent focused on the goal of plan A, you begin to make silent agreements, negotiate, and rationalize, 'It's ok if I fail or if plan A is too difficult, because I've always got plan B.'"

11

NO PLAN B

I have fought the good fight, I have finished the race, I have kept the faith.
—2 Timothy 4:7

When I was on active duty, I was asked all the time by people for "tips" on how to pass the Special Forces Assessment and Selection (SFAS). My answer was always the same and quite simple. Don't quit! The reaction was also always the same. "Seriously, come on, bro, what's the secret?" As if I was hiding some national security secret. Cat's out of the bag. That is the big secret. This is the most important lesson that will serve me well for the rest of my life. One may always be susceptible to self-assessment. One's mind may often tell you that you are not good enough. Stop listening to yourself and ignore those thoughts. Get out of your own head, take one task at a time, grind, and do not quit. This had to be my strategy to pass dive school as well.

I've heard it said that one can either quit or keep going, but both are hard. That is true, quitting has a little steeper pain. It's easy to become mentally defeated. It's easy to quit. The mind always wants to protect you. The mind does what the body prefers. It has been said that what we do and think originates in the mind. I believe that is only half correct. It starts in the mind as it is tied to the heart, the center of our emotions. Our hearts are the center of who we are. This is why Solomon tells us to "keep your heart with all vigilance for from it flows the springs of life" (Prov. 4:23). Nelson Mandela illuminates this thought when he said, "Don't talk to their minds; talk to their hearts." We must exercise caution then as the mind is deceitful in its motivations, thoughts, will, and emotional states and cannot always be trusted (Jeremiah 17:9). Because of this, it's been said, trust your gut, listen to your heart, and question your mind. Our hearts drive all we do, so we must make a habit of strengthening our hearts and minds, by what we meditate on.

I wasn't immune to quitting. There is always a not so small voice in the back of your mind questioning you: *Why are you doing this? Only a fool would go through this torture*. Other times, it would whisper subtly, *You should just quit*. In fact, I almost quit my second attempt at SFAS. It was January and our class got hit with a snowstorm. Cold weather gear was still not allowed. It was a mandatory part of our packing list, but we better not get caught wearing it.

The toughest event thus far and the event that produced the most failures from SFAS was the Star Course. All candidates followed the same packing list. Each equipped with a minimum of a fifty-five-pound rucksack with four quarts of water, dummy M-4, red lens, map of Camp Mackall, compass, protractor, pencil, and notebook.

The Star Course had started. Midnight came quickly and they allowed us to get about an hour of sleep. I received grid coordinates to my first point and began plotting my route. Bones Fork Creek. Its name doesn't do it justice, it is at least a stream, but seemed more like a lake without flowing water. Found in the swampiest area of Camp Mackall, it is hardly a creek. I couldn't believe it. I examined the map and looked for any possible route to reach my point without having to cross the creek. There was no such alternative solution. *Oh well, time to go and get it*, I thought!

I threw the big "heater" (rucksack) on my back and began jogging to my first point. Once I got to the creek, I looked for the best place to cross (where I wouldn't get as wet). My pant legs were already frozen from trudging through the snow. During our training iterations, we had already been introduced to Bones Fork Creek, which we affectionately called Scuba Road because the water was so deep. I had hoped that we would never meet again after those iterations. I stared at the only logical point to cross—straight across. All the other areas were thick with overgrowth. You could always know the depth of the water because there was a big wooden pole stuck in the middle of the water with a can on top of it. The water was nearly touching the can. That meant, the water would be well over my head. If I crossed, I would have to spend the next nine hours not only freezing, but soaking wet as well. As I stood there, I heard another candidate approaching. To keep my fifty-meter separation, I ran back into the wood line.

With no second thought, he ran right up and jumped in—splash! That didn't look like a good plan. I decided to take off my BDUs and socks, tie them to the top of my rucksack, fill my wet weather bag that lined my rucksack with air, so it would float, and cross naked, just wearing my boots. Miserable, yes, but at least I could put on dry clothes afterwards. When I approached the water, it was frozen. How could it be frozen if a candidate just crossed? It was that cold out. I broke the ice with my dummy rifle and swam across. On the other side, I put my clothes back on, shot my azimuth, and dead-reckoned to my first point.

The point sitter gave me my next grid coordinates. I was all the way at the bottom of the training area and I had to go all the way to the top of the training area. I was furious. We were told that the points were assigned at random, but I was starting to feel as if someone hated me. I walked back to Scuba Road and got naked again. Walking around with my heater on my back looking for the path I made when I crossed only ten minutes prior. It no longer existed. I was in shock, it had already frozen back over.

If I wanted to give myself a chance, I had to run the entire way to my second point. I found it without issue. It had to get easier from here. Not so much. My third point was where I just came from. It wasn't the same point, but it was only about 500 meters away. I plotted and replotted several times because this couldn't be right. We all hoped we wouldn't get Scuba Road as one of the points, but to get it not only once, but twice? Someone certainly hated me!

I was floored, at this rate I was going to cover at least fifty kilometers over the ten hours. Not only did I have to go all the way from the top of the training area to the very bottom, but I had to get naked and cross Scuba Road for the third and fourth time. At this point, I was starting to get miserable. When I got back to Scuba Road, I was questioning myself. What was I doing? Is it worth it? Enough of these stupid games. It's too cold. I was shivering uncontrollably. I couldn't do it. I wasn't going to do it.

There was a candidate that had lit a fire in the woods. He constructed a Dakota Fire Hole, covered the flames and the smoke of the fire with a poncho, so as not to be detected. But my senses were heightened from being in the woods for so many days. My nose detected the faint smell of smoke and told me there was warmth to be had. The temptation kept calling. I felt faint of heart and in that moment, I would have given anything to quit. Instead, I prayed for strength. I was reminded of John 14:1 and prayed, "Let not your hearts be troubled." Encouraged by God's word, I was not willing to exchange the temporary comfort from the fire for the chance to be selected to train to become a Green Beret.

Back in dive school, we were all battle proven and combat veterans. We had already proven that we were smart and tough enough to be in Special Forces, but one's Special Forces and Ranger Tabs were of no use here as the water became a great equalizer and our hearts would again be measured. Combat diver students vow they will die before quitting, but in the end, land could not teach the resolve beyond mental and physical limits such as the water can and many end up quitting, giving in to seemingly good reasons to quit. Wife is pregnant, "It's not for me", missing home after multiple deployments, medical issues, etc. It was the cadre's job to find reasons to get us to consider quitting in the pool. Better to find out who would quit in the pool rather than in a real world life-or-death situation.

The mental anguish began to supersede the physical anguish. I don't believe that our failures are final. They are often necessary stepping stones to success.

Yet, the cost of quitting in special operations has final failure implications indeed. Once a person voluntarily withdraws from training, a special mark is placed by their name in their file indicating they quit, and they are never allowed to return to try again. So, when the mind begins to look for excuses to quit, deceiving us by telling us that we have reached total exhaustion long before we reached our physical limit, we need to shut it up. You can't completely turn off your brain, but it is necessary to search deep to find the part of your brain that is screaming at you to quit and turn it off.

It took a lot to convince my company leadership, but they cut me travel orders to attend the very next dive school class. Most people that fail the course, take between four to six months to shake off the failure, regroup, and retrain. I didn't have that luxury. Only two months had passed since our deployment to Afghanistan, and my team was already preparing to deploy to Colombia. We were tasked with training the Colombian police's SWAT teams. We also had a separate follow-on mission to train their Colombian Navy SEALS. All my friends from my team had graduated and were wearing their bubbles. The deal was, I would have my final opportunity to pass dive school and then pass or fail, immediately fly to South America to catch up with my team and get back on mission.

I had less than a month to prepare to go back to dive school. I was already in excellent shape, but I was mentally and physically exhausted. I didn't have much of a break in the last year. From Afghanistan, we rolled into pre-scuba, and from pre-scuba into dive school. I needed a vacation, but that wasn't an option. I didn't want anything to do with the water, so I stayed out of it. During the three weeks leading up to my return to dive school, I only ran and lifted weights.

The month in between my classes passed quickly. Boarding my flight back to school was different from the previous flight. My first flight to dive school, I traveled with three teammates and three from Bravo company's dive team that I had gone through pre-scuba with; however, this one I traveled only with the constant reminder of my previous failure. The SF community is small, so I landed and took my taxi to the compound, and checked in, it turned out that I knew several people in the course after all. No one wanted to think of the start of the course the next morning. We weren't allowed to drive in Key West, so we all had to rent beach cruisers to get around in Key West. Once all our admin stuff was completed, we rode our bikes downtown and customarily ate a fine meal. There was lots of nervous laughter, but it was good. All of our minds were kept off of the pain that would ensue the very next morning as we entered the hallowed testing ground. We were aware that pre-scuba was able to weed out some of the carnage of dive school, but it couldn't flawlessly predict which one of us would not graduate CDQC.

The start time is 5 AM. No instructor comes to yell at you to get you out of bed. It behooved us to be at the right place at the right time from here on out. The course started with the PT test and was followed by two mandatory pass/fail events to get in the course—the fifty-meter subsurface swim and the 100-meter freestyle swim around the perimeter of the pool in full uniform. In Olympic swimming, the fifty-meter freestyle is the fastest event. At dive school, the fifty-meter subsurface swim is not about speed. Completed on a single breath, it is about form.

Beginning in the shallow end, the technique is to submerge your body from the shoulders down. It is less dependent on the technique though and more about do you have the heart and will to be comfortable being uncomfortable. Taking several long deep breaths and with one last giant inhale, go subsurface. As you begin the twenty-five-meter swim to the wall, the goal is to remain as low as possible to the pool floor, reducing drag. I was so low that I could hear the metal buckle from my UDT (Underwater Demolition Team) shorts scraping the floor. Rather than kick frantically expending unnecessary energy, you must maximize both the pull of your arms and the kick of your legs, propelling you forward and gliding as far as possible. Swimmers must find ways to minimize the resistance of their body in the water. That's why the professional swimmers you see are clean-shaven from head to toe. Water resistance is also affected by a person's size and shape. *Forward-Driving Force – Resistance = Velocity* is the winning formula for preventing a hypoxic blackout during this exercise. USA Swimming and the American Red Cross have defined hypoxic blackout (also known as shallow water blackout) as "the loss of consciousness in the swimmer or diver, during an apnea submersion preceded by hyperventilation, where alternative causes of unconsciousness have been excluded." This can happen at any water depth.

There was no time limit for the 100-meter swim, just don't touch the sides or the bottom. For the cost of the plane ticket down to Key West and being a Green Beret, you better not fail the PT test and these entry-level skills!

There were two phases of the course. The pool phase and the dive phase. The dream was to make it to the dive phase, but the pool phase was the evil gatekeeper to the dive phase. You had to master the basics of combat swimming in the pool before being granted permission to be on air in the ocean. The days of pool phase were divided into four parts: the morning run, pool training, classroom instruction, and ocean swims.

It was Zero Week, better known as Hell Week. This week we weren't taught much. We spent most of it getting scuffed up. The energy zapping started with the requirement to run everywhere you went during the day. If you were moving from one place to another, you better be running, have your dive buddy and your one gallon, half-Gatorade, half-Water jug with you. Constantly being in motion throughout the day quickly compounds your fatigue.

As a Green Beret and Ranger, I was always trained to have a plan B. Actually, I was trained to have several backup plans. We developed redundancy into all our mission planning, to ensure when the primary plan failed the mission would not fail. We called this framework our PACE plan—Primary, Alternate, Contingency, and Emergency. Our contingencies went four levels deep.

But this time, I could not have a plan B. I went in with the mindset of I had no other options but to complete the course. Having a plan B while pursuing goals makes it possible to quit. Having a plan B requires splitting energy from plan A. Having a plan B is simply a distraction from your primary goal. Instead of being 100 percent focused on the goal of plan A, you begin to make silent agreements, negotiate, and rationalize, "It's ok if I fail or if plan A is too difficult, because I've always got plan B." Having volunteered to be there, it was time for the cadre to see exactly who wanted to be there. I had been there before, and I had no plan B. I was all in!

Hurrrry... UP! Which one of you is the weak link? If you are weak, go home! These and other less repeatable statements were shouted at us as we entered single file through the narrow gate opening of the fence and onto the pool deck. We were all experienced operators. All students in this class had already earned their Green Beret and many had started their career as Rangers as well. We were beyond getting yelled at! We were used to being treated as professionals by this point in our careers. What made it more frustrating was the cadre were our peers. When they were done with their two-to-three-year assignment, they would filter back into the community. The important difference—they were qualified to wear the coveted Combat Diver Qualification Diver's badge (dive bubble). The dive instructors are dressed in khaki shorts, black t-shirts, and black hats. Similar to the jumpmasters in Airborne School, their black hats had two pins on the front of it, their rank, and their dive bubble.

No matter how fast we moved, it was never fast enough. We were always given some absurd time standard that was impossible to meet. This was purposeful. We would get scuffed up and "smoked" on the sacred pool deck daily, and our legs and lungs would be burning long before ever entering the pool. Although difficult, the events were passable in and of themselves. It was terrifying to jump in the pool having already completed a long run that morning. Our legs, hip flexors, and abs all felt like rubber and had the tensile strength of a jellyfish from the hundreds of flutter kicks performed prior to our four-hour daily pool sessions.

We had to take one event at a time. It has been said about distance running, to run the mile you are in. While experiencing the current punishment, letting your mind drift for even a second to think about what was left in the daily schedule was always a costly mistake. At this heightened sense of danger to the body, the mind was always lying to you and whispering in your ear, "Just quit… all you have to do is quit and all the pain will stop immediately. It's not worth it, no one will blame you." I needed to block out the noise of this senseless self-chatter to focus on the task at hand. What is the noise in your life that you need to block out? Don't be concerned with what people think of you. Do not be bothered by social media posts. Take charge and develop the ability to block out all that is irrelevant.

Our winter dive class entered the gate to the pool deck, where the cadre waited for us like a lion waits for its prey. We belonged to the cadre for the next four hours. As we entered, we immediately became victim to their yelling, so as to put us in duress and panic. From day one of the course, we were training to avoid panic because panic in dangerous situations is what often kills divers rather than the danger itself. Then out comes the hose. The venomous bite from the cold water hitting me immediately snatched the air out of my lungs. The water was irritating, but I hated the cold. I didn't really mind being cold or wet, but I hated being cold and wet. It was January in Key West and the average morning temperature in Key West is about 68 degrees. Even though the weather could get up to 70+ degrees, the water temperature only ranged from mid to high 60s. To the non-diver that may not sound cold, but when you are being sprayed with water from all four cardinal directions it gets cold quickly. So cold that it is possible to become hypothermic in this water temperature.

It was essential not to show that you were bothered by the water. Having any type of reaction to the cold water and you became blood in the water and the shark cadre were going to immediately identify you and exploit your weakness. Prior to our arrival the gear that we staged on the deck prior to PT was inspected. Attention to detail was vital, if one person had a mistake, any mistake at all, we would all pay for it. We would enter the deck to find our gear scattered all over, to include the bottom of the pool.

"On your backs, men!" We became very familiar with the flutter kick exercise. "In cadence… exercise. One, two, three, ONE, one, two, three, TWO..." As we lay on the deck and exercised, the instructors would "charge" (fill with water) our masks. As the instructors flooded our masks with water, the cold water was no longer a concern. Our dive masks covered our noses, so we could only breathe through our mouths. Having knowledge of this, the cadre sprayed our mouths. With every breath of air we were also inhaling water. This is not a fun experience, quite frankly, it's what drowning feels like. This was a brutal, but vital skill to learn. You had to learn to breathe around the water and gain the experiential understanding that you wouldn't die from inhaling water. That is, if you kept your wits about you and didn't panic. It wasn't what the instructors inflicted on us that mattered. What mattered was how we chose to deal with it.

Being comfortable with this was an important part of the training as each year a leading cause of civilian death is caused by the ensuing panic of water inhalation underwater. This type of training was the beginning of making us confident and able to handle any emergency that came our way. It may be possible to pass dive school if you are a weak swimmer, but it is impossible to defeat a fear of the water without being comfortable and familiar with it.

We couldn't do anything right and now found ourselves with our masks and fins on at the edge of the pool. As we hovered our extended legs six inches above the surface of the water, our bodies shivered uncontrollably. "Oh you guys are cold? No problem, I have something for you, in cadence exercise." Our shivering bodies began to heat up as we flutter kicked. These were not ordinary military flutter kicks. With each kick our fins had to break the surface of the water. With the added weight of the water, pulling our fins back above the surface was exhausting and set our ab muscles on fire. This torture too was a vital part of the training. Flutter kicks developed our core and hip flexor muscles that were needed to perform successful dive operations.

This was only the beginning. It was the intent of the cadre to physically exhaust us daily. Before we even entered the water, every muscle fiber in my legs was set on fire. Each additional exercise was purposely designed to push students to their limits. At any time during the daily four hours of torture in the pool there was always the bell. The brass bell was deliberately positioned so that it was always in the students' view. You weren't being forced to complete the training, you volunteered to attend. Nobody was going to try to change your mind. When you'd reached utter exhaustion and simply had enough, all you had to do to quit was get out of the pool, walk over, and ring the bell. When rung, the sound echoes throughout the training area, announcing another student has *voluntarily withdrawn.*

The act of ringing the bell has a diverse history. During the Middle Ages, the ringing of the bell marked significant events such as weddings, was used to warn of danger, or was used to simply mark the time of day. I have seen a few instances today where the ringing of the bell has a positive connotation. While sitting inside an Arby's restaurant, I cringe seeing the bell hanging parallel to the exit door with the intent of patrons ringing it on their way out to signify good service and satisfaction with their meal. Georgia Tech has a time-honored tradition of ringing the bell to celebrate graduates of their MBA program. At oncology institutions across the nation, it has become common for patients to ring the bell to mark the milestone of completing their last treatment. Ringing the bell, while acceptable in other places, is never an option in our environment.

While others were struggling with the taunting of the cadre, "Make it easy on yourselves and quit," mentally I was prepared for everything they could throw at me. Part of the challenge is not knowing what is coming and just how much pain and suffering you can take. Having been there before, I knew I could take it all and then some. So much that I could laugh at it the second time around. The pain couldn't last forever. But it was still grueling, and I still had to complete it.

During the pool phase of dive school, the afternoon ocean swims become progressively longer. The final distance is a two-mile navigation swim where you are scored on speed and accuracy. At this distance, with choppy waves, the shoreline becomes difficult, sometimes impossible to see. This is an uneasy feeling, but beyond those two miles of discomfort is a new breakthrough where you will begin to know experientially just what you are truly capable of. You must be bold to explore new depths and distances. The only way to do that is by losing sight of the shore.

As the boat motored out, the smell of the ocean and intermittent spray of salt water on my face triggered memories of my time on the Florida beaches as a kid. I was suspended in time, saturated in blissful contentment. The boat slowed, the engine cut, and as we repositioned ourselves to mount the gunnel, I was brought back to the present. The momentary bliss was immediately replaced by anxiety as my stress response kicked in and cortisol, the stress hormone, began to circulate throughout my body. I could mentally quit, giving in to the stress, or overcome the activated stress response and fin as hard and as fast as I could to complete the two-mile swim.

Day by day the cadre continued to call my name, taunting me to quit, but no matter the misery, I couldn't give them the satisfaction. My mental strength began to compound, and I began to believe that the only way for them to get me out of this school was to kick me out or with a bloodstained dive bubble on my chest.

Application:

God did not create us to be defeated. We were not designed to quit. We may get pushed down, but we were not meant to stay there. We may get depressed, but we must not quit. Our hearts may be broken, but we cannot not give up. We must persevere in the face of illness. The unthinkable may strike, but we must not quit. Decide to win. You don't succeed merely because you didn't quit, but the only way to succeed is not to quit. Choose not to quit because you do not have a plan B. When we refuse to quit, God will bless us.

"There are only two honorable ways to leave dive school. One is by completing the course to standard and receiving your (dive bubble). The other is in a body bag."

12

BODY BAG OR BUBBLE

The six-week course is by far the most challenging in the Army. It is a course designed to find soldiers that would rather die in the pool than quit. You can't take a knee when you are tired in the ocean. The current will chew you up and spit you out. This course was more challenging for different reasons than Ranger School or the Q Course. This was by no means a gentlemen's course. We were exhausted, but at least the lack of food and sleep weren't a part of the training process. In fact, one of the hidden secrets of dive school is that it has one of the best chow halls (dining facilities) in the Army. We were gifted in knowing a few things: the food was ample and delicious and at some point each day, the training would end, and the remaining time was your own. I was up every night studying dive physics until ten or eleven. Ample food portions or not, I had still lost fifteen pounds over the course of only three weeks.

There are only two honorable ways to leave dive school. One is by completing the course to standard and receiving your (dive bubble). The other is in a body bag. When considering any other way, I had to ask myself what were the values that I wanted my kids to know that I stood for? When answering that question, the one inescapable thought was that I never wanted to look my children in the eye and explain to them that I quit something.

During the pool phase we practiced daily events that we would have to pass to exit and move on to the dive phase. One of those events was "ditch and don". I had practiced this event every day for nearly two weeks, and it was now time to test out. As I entered the water equipped with my buoyancy compensator device, sixteen-pound weight belt, mask, and fins, the instructor would purposefully take his time to give me instructions while I treaded water. As mentioned, treading water with no hands is not an easy task for me especially with a sixteen-pound weight belt. During the train up, I made the mistake of showing a little bit of stress the first day. The instructor noticed and took his sweet time getting through the instructions. On test day, I would not make that mistake again. Well acquainted with the rigors of the upcoming tasks, it was easy to allow my heart rate to elevate with anticipation, but I had to remain calm and try to keep my heart rate down prior to going subsurface. As I returned the dive signal to the instructor, I took one last deep breath and executed a flawless dolphin kick to propel me to the bottom of the nine-foot pool. With the gift of negative buoyancy (in this case), it was easy to get to the bottom having spent very little energy.

I pinched my nose and blew air through my nostrils to clear and equalize the pressure in my ears. Now the clock was ticking. I had to ditch my fins, weight belt, and mask. The difficulty was that each piece of equipment had to be perfectly aligned. Many made the mistake of after checking their gear alignment, kicking hard too close to their equipment during their ascent and pushing it out of alignment. As I made my assent to surface, the instructor watched to ensure I blew bubbles out continuously with no interruption. As I broke the surface fist first. The instructor asked, "How do you feel?" and I replied, "I feel fine," while giving him the OK signal. Minus a weight belt, there was momentary relief, but my heart rate was steadily climbing from the initial underwater breath hold.

As I treaded water, the instructor again took his time to drag his instructions out, explaining to me exactly how he was going to go and examine my gear. I was poised on the outside, but inside, I was screaming, "Shut up, get down there, and check my gear already." When the instructor returned from checking my gear, I was relieved to receive the approval to return subsurface and retrieve my gear. There are many techniques and really no wrong way of doing it. I preferred to grab my weight belt first. This helps keep you from fighting not to float away from your gear. While many wasted precious seconds fidgeting trying to get the belt into the clasp, a prior student had cut the edge of the belt diagonally to make it easier to insert, saving me time. Once my weight belt was secured, I laid on my back and checked the belt to make sure there weren't twists and that the buckle was securely fastened. I have seen plenty of weight belts slide off during the ascent of this exercise. While on my back, I put my fins on. This was an arduous task, requiring jamming my ill-fitting dive booties into my fins. Pulling the backstrap up around the ankle required a lot of effort. I wanted my fins to fit tight, so they didn't loosen during some of the other exercises. The preferred technique for this exercise was to loosen them a little bit, but the day had moved by so quickly between events, that I had no time.

Piece of cake. Having completed this exercise a myriad of times, I could feel that I was ahead of schedule based on my internal clock. I had worked on mastering my breath holds as a kid and always took pride in the ability to remain comfortable holding my breath underwater. In essence, I had trained for this exact moment unknowingly my entire life, but at this point, I stopped thinking about passing the event. My thoughts had shifted to surviving the event. But failure was out of the question, so my hope was to do both: survive and pass the event.

But wait, it wasn't a piece of cake. I couldn't find my mask. I looked left, I looked right. I looked up, I looked down—there was no mask. I laid on my back and with the sun magnified in my eyes, I could not see the mask floating anywhere. The instructor had to be messing with me. The instructor with snorkel in mouth was perfectly neutral buoyant and was floating over me in the distance with his arms crossed. I looked at him with my hands open as in, *I know you have it, give it back*. He looked back, opened his hands, and shrugged his shoulders.

As the carbon dioxide built up in my lungs, I off-gassed slightly, letting a small number of bubbles seep out of my mouth. A technique used to trick the brain into feeling as if I had taken an actual breath, extending my time before I blacked out. I could not do this too much. I needed to save enough air to later clear my mask and maintain exhaling bubbles on my ascent back to the surface.

The clock was my enemy as I searched for my mask. My sympathetic nervous system was highly activated and was causing my heart rate to begin to race. The longer I stayed down there, the closer I was to meeting the wizard. I was working too hard and burning a lot of time and, more importantly, oxygen. My lungs were burning and demanding immediate oxygen. I had to stay relaxed. The rise in my alpha wave brain activity increased my serotonin levels, allowing me to relax and enter a flow state. In the flow state I lost all awareness of time. Time no longer mattered. Forgetting I was submerged nine feet underwater, I moved from the solo thought of survival to focusing on the task at hand—recovering my equipment. This moment in time felt like I was somewhere between a dream and reality. In this state, I was able to decrease my heart rate and control my body like never before.

Back on my knees, I spun 360 degrees to the right and then 360 to the left. I had no time for this silly game. I thought that the mask had floated away, so I looked for it off in the distance. The water is kept in perfect condition. The proper pH balance and chlorine levels makes the water crystal clear with no eye irritation. I could see nearly the length of the pool. Running out of time, I ran my hands across my back and there it was. It was routed through my weight belt. I was running out of breath.

I had perfected passing this exercise with just enough time before running out of air. Losing my mask had added over a minute to my routine. Out of breath, but not out of time. It was time to finish the work.

I have no concept of how long I was under the water, but I remember it was long enough for everyone to stop what they were doing and focus solely on me. All other training stopped, fully expecting the need to deploy all medical personnel in my direction. As I began my ascent, I believed I didn't have enough air to continuously expel. To complicate it further, I couldn't ascend faster than my slowest bubble. This was training to protect myself from a dive-related injury. Ascend too fast during a dive and the nitrogen bubbles won't have enough time to escape my body. Interrupting my exhale during a dive on compressed air, the expanding air could rupture lung tissue and release gas bubbles into the arteries—i.e., an arterial gas embolism.

These bubbles are extremely dangerous and could cause damage to the brain or even death. If I interrupted my exhalation during this exercise, the work up to that point was all for nothing. I recall the lights were dimming as I looked up, my right hand toward the surface and left hand securing my weight belt. As my hand broke the surface, I smiled as big as I could not because I was happy. I needed to break the seal of my mask and get any last droplets of water out. Once I swam to the gunnel, I would immediately be inspected for deficiencies. On the pool deck, an instructor inspected my mask. The other instructor ran his hands across the back of my weight belt ensuring there were no twists. Lifting my body higher onto the gunnel to expose my fins, he inspected my straps to make sure the buckles were properly seated and there again were no twists. *Roll!* I rolled carefully onto my back, making sure that I did not open the clasp of the weight belt before it was inspected. The never-ending event was over.

"Mr. Brown, what are the only two ways to leave dive school?"

I replied, "Body bag or Bubble, Dive Sup!" The pool deck erupted in cheers and in that moment everything changed. Moments earlier, I wanted to breathe. I wanted to quit, but quitting meant accepting defeat, proving everyone right, and giving up on a dream. I didn't quit. I was now in control. I was confident, nothing would stop me. Having experienced God's overwhelming peace—my belief had changed.

As exhiliarting as conquering this event was and having a taste of this mindset, it wouldn't be until two years later when I would meet Mark Maierson, that I would truly come to experientially understand this mindset of Body Bag or Bubble.

Marky

My flesh and my heart may fail, but God is the strength of my heart and my portion forever.
—Psalm 73:26

Thirty-five Green Berets started my dive school class and less than twenty of us finished. The *Body Bag or Bubble* mindset carried me through the rest of dive school. In February 2007, I completed the rigorous six weeks of training, including the ocean navigation dives and the final Field Training Exercise, and graduated dive school. Each of the graduates lined up to shake the hands of the instructors and receive our dive bubble. The uniform was still our UDT shorts and brown t-shirt, but we added our ACU top to pin our award on. As the cadre shook my right hand, he handed me my bubble in the left. The tradition is to then hand the bubble back and the first instructor in line places the badge on your shirt without the backing, makes a fist, he then pounds the award into your chest. Each instructor thereafter takes their turn pounding their fist on top of your award—this is known as receiving your blood bubble. After the quick pinning ceremony, I said my goodbyes and raced to the airport enroute back to Fort Bragg. This flight was much different than the last flight home. Instead of thinking of my failure, I was thinking about my accomplishment. I was grateful to God. Though I had put in a lot of physical and mental work, I was sure that it was God's hand that had sustained me.

After dive school, I went back to the team. I was now *on* the team, but the reality was my position was temporary. One of the things that keeps Special Forces "special" is that you must continue to contribute. When people become lax and take their foot off the gas, they will arrive at the team door and see their stuff thrown in the hallway. Bewildered and confused, no need to try the cipher lock and find out the combination has been changed because just like that you are off the team. I had to fight every day to remain on the team, bettering myself and those around me.

Most SF guys eventually are required to do rotations as instructors. As my career progressed, it was now time for me to rotate to the John F. Kennedy Special Warfare Center and School (SWCS) at Fort Bragg, NC, to serve as an instructor. No one wants to leave the team. At the same time, my unit was looking for volunteers for the developmental canine program. No one had many answers to my questions about the program. I was told that I would be able to return to my team to employ the capability. I was sold, I volunteered for training to avoid the schoolhouse and stay engaged with my team becoming one of the first Special Operations Forces Multi-Purpose Canine (SOFMPC) handlers for 7th SFG.

I completed the canine training, but instead of returning to my team, I became an asset for the entire group. When we deployed stateside for PMT, I finagled my way back onto my old ODA and petitioned to be attached with this ODA during our deployment. Green Berets trust themselves and their training. Being attached to a random team that didn't know me would have proven more difficult to engage the new canine capability into missions. When we arrived in Afghanistan, the team was short an 18C because I was technically no longer on the team. A third of the way into the deployment, Mark Maierson arrived as my replacement as the second 18C on the ODA. This is where Mark and I became close friends.

Mark was a great guy. It's not easy to be on our team, but he quickly grew to fit right in. He was a PT stud and he knew his job. He also had a humble heart and wasn't afraid to ask for help. Remembering how difficult my first deployment was with this crew, not having my dive bubble, I decided to take him under my wing and walk alongside him ensuring his experience was better than mine. During this deployment, he became like a little brother to me. We had both been through a lot up to that point in our lives. We confided in one another and often talked about opening a future photography business together. This helped kill time and gave us something to hope for amid the confines of war.

After we redeployed to Fort Bragg, we trained Mark up for dive school. Mark was an endurance monster. He was a small guy, but a physical beast. He broke ten minutes in the two-mile run, but could also bench press over 300 pounds. For every other guy that I trained, I sent them off knowing they had a 50/50 chance of passing. Mark was a natural in the water. I was confident he was ready. Before he left, I shook his hand and told him I knew he would crush the course and I looked forward to diving with him when he returned. Even though I had a few more conversations with Mark checking in with him weekly at dive school, that was the last time I would see my friend.

There is only one name that comes to mind that truly embodied this mindset of Body Bag or Bubble. That name is Staff Sergeant Mark Maierson. On March 13, 2009, standing on the pool deck at the Special Forces Underwater Operations School in Key West, Florida, looking at the calm, still, blue water, with a burst of adrenaline surging through him, SSG Maierson holding his mask with his right hand and weight belt with his left, he looked left, looked right, and returned his head to look center, and waited for the command to enter the water. At the command, he took one giant step forward simultaneously with his fellow trainees to enter the water. Immediately beginning to fin, he was brought back to the surface and with head and hands out of the water, he began what would be the final tank tread exercise of his life.

While conducting the tank tread exercise, Mark lost consciousness, his body went limp, and with 100 pounds of gear on his back he sank to the bottom of the pool. Eyewitnesses say the medical team got him out of the pool immediately and began rescue breathing. But when they pulled Mark to the surface, he was already blue. It didn't make sense. The medical team tried to revive him. He was then rushed to the Lower Keys Medical center, but at the age of twenty-seven years, only six years into his military career, my best friend was pronounced dead, and I would never get to dive with him. Even though the most minute oversight could be a fatal mistake, I am more than confident, the medical team did everything right that day.

It's likely Mark's heart stopped beating long before his legs stopped finning. He had resolved not to quit, even when his heart had failed, he continued to fight with all of his might. Knowing him well, he had an intangible trait—intestinal fortitude that allowed him to push past the pain, push past the point of exhaustion, and would not allow him to quit. Even at the expense of his life. SSG Maierson embodied the mantra, *B*ody *B*ag or *B*ubble.

No soldier can give more to his country than his life. Mark was a hero, somebody we all aspired to be. Even before his passing, he had become a hero to us. He had both the heart of a servant and that of a warrior. Daily we saw that he was willing to do what was right and fight to protect it. I never got to dive in the open water with Mark. We never got to continue our daydreams about the future while prepping our dive gear, with the soundtrack of the ocean roaring in the background. As I write this, fifteen years later, his death still does not make sense, but we are at peace knowing that his final breath on earth was not his last, but instead he is now resting in Heaven, and we will meet again.

Application:

Stop settling for the safe version of your life that's easily attainable and start chasing the seemingly impossible dream. There is greatness inside of you. Are you willing to do all that it is required to unlock your potential and achieve your dream or die before giving up? Begin living the Body Bag or Bubble mindset. Then and only then, will you be able to achieve your true potential.

"Earning the Special Forces Combat Diver Badge is not easy no matter the color of your skin, but I am proof that it is not impossible either. As it turns out, black people can swim!"

13

BOAT'S ON FIRE

There were many games the instructors put us through in the pool. Standing on the side of the pool, waiting next to our gear bags for our next instructions, we noticed our tanks were sitting on the bottom of the pool. Then one of the instructors yelled, "*Boats on fire!*" And they began launching our gear bags into the pool. *Boats on fire! Get in the water!* We only had seconds to react and get into the pool.

Once in the pool without gear, you immediately began to appreciate every piece of equipment. The task was to find our gear and put it into function. If you came up for air before attaching your regulator to your tanks—that's right, you guessed it—you fail! It was important to stay calm and relaxed during the chaos, but success during this *game* was achieved well before the game began. Success was achieved in the preparation. If you prepared properly then, your necessary gear was organized in your bag, your bag was buttoned closed, and your gear remained in your bag when they tossed it, making it easy to locate and to make operational.

The ultimate test of staying calm during chaos is the One-Man Competency Exam. It is the capstone of the pool phase and is the mandatory requirement to begin the dive phase of training. Everyone dreaded this exam. It wasn't your typical exam requiring pencil and paper. Instead, you were given a blacked-out mask, two fully equipped twin-eighty tanks, and placed on your knees at the bottom of the pool. With the blacked-out mask, students are required to perform all skills in total darkness, during the twenty-minute exam. Throughout this period, the instructors observe your every move.

Throughout the exam, students are brought through a series of events. After the first five minutes of simulating an ocean surge, the instructors begin to remove the air source from the students. Trained to focus on recovering their air source, students are now tested on their ability not to panic and maintain focus on recovering the air source. During dives, the men are connected by several lines. If one person panics and shoots to the surface too fast, it could kill not only the individual diver, but the entire team causing them to have an arterial gas embolism.

The last phase of the exercise is the unrecoverable air source. This portion of the test demands concentration. The instructor takes both your regulator and LPI hose and ties it in a knot that is only able to be untied by removing your tanks. By this point in the exercise, you are nearly hypoxic and about fifteen to twenty seconds from blacking out. Once a student is able to pass this rigorous test, they are confident the student can dive in the open ocean.

The lessons learned from successfully completing One-Man Comp are vital, but they do not directly transfer to the sea because the unforgiving nature of the sea cannot be simulated in a pool. One-Man Comp taught me not to fight the water. There is no amount of intelligence or strength that can aid you in defeating the water. The water is an undefeatable monster. It is our ego that makes us think that we can fight and overpower the water. It offers no weak points for you to exploit. To be successful in One-Man Comp, you must learn to relax and submit to the water's rhythm, allowing its flow to work for you, then address one problem at a time. During the exercise, the instructors are throwing several problems at you at one time. Trying to tackle them all at once is a mistake. You must decide which are the most urgent and begin solving them in the order or precedence.

Application:

Do you stay prepared daily in the event the chaos of *the boats on fire* may come?

Head Back and Breathe

So we do not lose heart. Though our outer self is wasting away, our inner self is being renewed day by day. For this light momentary affliction is preparing for us an eternal weight of glory beyond all comparison, as we look not to the things that are seen but to the things that are unseen. For the things that are seen are transient, but the things that are unseen are eternal.
—2 Corinthians 4:16-18

Eric Thomas, a.k.a. the Hip Hop Preacher, is famous for saying, "When you want to succeed as bad as you want to breathe, then you'll be successful." But success won't happen overnight. So, what do we do in those times of frustration and disappointment while waiting for our breakthrough?

As we chase our dreams, there are moments where we may become discouraged, weary, fainthearted, and our capacity whittles down to barely running on fumes. In these moments, it may seem impossible to get off the emotional rollercoaster.

When it seemed like there were no other options, dive school taught me to simply breathe. Lined up in the pool waiting for our next event, the instructors would yell, "Head back and breathe." Cognitive scientists have proven that the sounds of water are calming to the brain. As we tilted our heads back to open the airway and took that exact moment to consciously breathe deeply, we began to be renewed. The slow inhale and exhale pace of controlled breathing soothed us.

How we breathe affects everything. James Nestor in his book, *Breath*, says that, "Breathing is so much more than getting air into our bodies. It's the most intimate connection to our surroundings… to breathe is to absorb ourselves in what surrounds us, to take in little bits of life, understand them, and give pieces of ourselves back out."[18] There is spiritual power connected to breathing. God Himself is not silent when it comes to breath. Breath is very important to Him. It was through His very breath that He breathed His Word into man. Job records that, "The Spirit of God has made me and the breath of the Almighty gives me life" (Job 33:4).

Whether you are in the military and living in an environment with a constant high operational tempo or in business and trying to succeed while dealing with the disappointments along the way, life is brutal, and it wears you down. At some point we all become tired and overwhelmed. These are reminders that we all need rest for our souls. God in His kindness sent His Son Jesus to provide us rest that deep breathing can't offer. When you feel you have no more strength to carry on, Jesus offers complete healing to those who have sinned, failed, and suffered. As we experience

---

[18] Nestor, James. *Breath: The New Science of a Lost Art.* Riverhead Books, 2021.

painful struggles to endure, He carries us along by His grace. Faith in Jesus offers perfect rest, so that we do not lose heart.

Burn the Ships

I have fought the good fight, I have finished the race, I have kept the faith.
—2 Timothy 4:7

I began the journey needing to see (no pun intended) what the water could teach me about pushing past my assumed limits and conquering my fears. But graduating dive school is not the most important part of my story. My story is bigger than my sole pursuit to achieve something. It's about the lessons learned through the process of becoming a Special Forces Combat Diver. In the water, my heart and mind were tested (Psalm 26:2), and the process of the pursuit led to a deeper understanding of not only what my mind was capable of, but of exactly who God is.

It brought me to the end of myself and experientially caused me to rely on God. When my mind was telling me to panic, I felt His peace through me. When I was tempted to be afraid, I was reminded He is with me wherever I was (Joshua 1:9; Isaiah 41:10). It truly was an opportunity not to trust in my own heart, but to lean on the Lord. During difficult times, people draw strength and build resilience from different things, but I can say with confidence that "my flesh and my heart may fail, God is the strength of my heart and my portion forever (Psalm 73:26).

When I earned my dive bubble, I was the only black diver in my unit. Before I left 7th Special Forces Group, I had the honor of putting others through pre-scuba and watching them graduate dive school and earn their bubbles as well. True leadership embodies growth of others around you. Earning the Special Forces Combat Diver Badge is not easy no matter the color of your skin, but I am proof that it is not impossible either. As it turns out, black people can swim! Against all odds and people telling me that I couldn't do it—if I was able to conquer dive school, there's hope for you. Our accomplishments are only limited by our ability to dream. Dream big! Go do what you were told was impossible. Do not give up on your dream simply because someone told you can't do something.

There are some reading this book who may be experiencing real problems right now. Who may be going through a difficult time handling past or even present failure. Every difficulty we face is related to our concept of God. Our difficulties will be small if we view God as big, and every challenge will be an opportunity. If our view of God is small, then our problems will appear to be large and insurmountable. I encourage you to turn to the Lord. The Lord upholds all who fall (Psalm 145:14). Thank God, we can experience this restoration by trusting Him. Consider this picture of David's experience of grace, forgiveness, and being made new in Psalms: "He lifted me out of the slimy pit, out of the mud and mire; he set my feet on a rock and gave me a firm place to stand. He put a new song in my mouth, a hymn of praise to our God. Many will see and fear the Lord and put their trust in him" (40:2-3). God is a present help in times of failure and is ready to extend His forgiveness for those who place their trust in Him.

In 1519, Hernan Cortes arrived at Vera Cruz with a small force of 600 men. He gathered his exhausted men on the beach and gave the order to burn the ships, destroying their way of escape. His men watched the boats sink into the Gulf of Mexico. With no way of retreat, they only had one choice: to push forward and succeed. God's will for your life is the only choice. Whatever goal you are chasing, whatever you have been called to do that seems impossible, you too must purposefully set fire to all options of escape. It's time to stop making excuses about making excuses and resolve in your heart that there is no plan B. Whatever the cost of following God and achieving what He has called you to do, you must be willing to pay it above all else.

Burn the ships!

APPENDIX

History Timeline

1831 – Tice Davids swam to freedom from slavery across the Ohio River.

1868 – The nation's first municipal pool was built in Boston, MA.

1920s – All-black swim teams began to appear throughout the US.

1926 – The federal government mandated racial segregation of pools in Washington, D.C.

1931 – The first National Colored Swimming Championship was held in Washington, D.C.

1950 – The federal government desegregated public swimming pools in Washington, D.C.

1948 – Military was desegregated.

1954 – Carl Brashear completed US Navy Diving & Salvage Training, becoming the first African American to attend and graduate from the school and the first American US Navy diver.

1967 – Fred Rogers and Officer Francois Clemmons soaked their feet in the kiddie pool.

1970 – Carl Brashear became first US Navy Master Diver.

1971 – Jim Ellis formed the Philadelphia Department of Recreation (or, "Pride, Determination, Resilience") Swim Team in Pennsylvania.

1975 – Sabir Muhammad became the first black swimmer to hold an American record.

1982 – Chris Silva became the first black swimmer to make a US National Team.

1988 – Sybil Smith became the first female black swimmer to score in a NCAA final.

1988 – Anthony Nesty became the first black swimmer to win an Olympic gold medal, the first to win an individual World Championship, and NCAA Division 1 Championship.

2004 – Maritza Correia McClendon became the first black female swimmer to make the US Olympic Team and win a silver medal.

2006 – Cullen Jones became the first black swimmer to break a world record in the 4x100m relay.

2015 – Three black swimmers, Simone Manuel, Lia Neal, and Natalie Hinds sweprt first, second, and third place in the NCAA Swimming Championship.

2016 – Anthony Ervin won Olympic gold in the fifty-meter freestyle.

2016 – Simone Manuel became the first black woman to win an individual Olympic gold in swimming and set an Olympic and American record

2024 – Anthony Nesty appointed as the first black US Olympic head swimming coach.

TRIBUTE TO FALLEN COMBAT DIVERS

SFC Louis S. Pall - SFUWO Instructor	Died 1969 on MFF DZ
2LT William Koscher - HHC 7th SFG(A).	Died 8/15/1969 in Key West, FL
SP4 John A. James - A Co, 3rd SFG(A)	Died 8/15/1969 in Key West, FL
CSM Raymond L. Long - 3rd BDE, 101st ABN	KIA 5/6/1970 Vietnam
SRA Mark L. Crockford - USAF Pararescue	Died 6/10/1981 DZ in North Sea
SSGT Justin Y. Jones - 41st Aerospace Rescue &Rec Sqn)	Died 4/11/1983 Pacific Ocean pilot rescue site
SFC Terry L. Gilden - HHC, USASOC	KIA 4/18/1983 Lebanon
SGT Randy E. Cline - A/1/75	KIA 10/25/1983 in Grenada
SSGT Eddy D. Clark - CCT	Died 2/28, 1984 Spain
SGT Jonathon E. Goerling - CCT	Died 2/28/1984 Spain

A1C James A. Ferreira - USAF Pararescue	Died 4/7/1984 Cape Canaveral, FL
SGT Robert A. Jermyn - USAF Pararescue	Died 1/20/1985 Hickman AFB, HI
SSGT Robert W. Kimbrel - 1550th TSCTS	Died 4/2/1986 Kirtland AFB, NM
TSGT Wayne R. Jones - 342nd TRS	Died 9/27/1988 Nellis AFB, NV
SGT Robert Reyes - 2nd Force RECON CO	Died 10/22/1988 on MFF DZ, Ft. Pickett, VA
MSG John M. Yancey, Jr. - HHC, USASOC	Died 1989 on Rng 19, Ft. Bragg, NC
CPT Randi L. Horstman - ODA 155	Died 10/17/1989 in Seoul, Korea
SFC Kevin L. Devorak - B/2/1 SFG(A)	Died 10/18/1990 Key West, FL
SGM Patrick R. Hurley - HHC, USASOC	KIA 2/21/1991 Saudi Arabia
MSG Eloy A. Rodriguez - HHC, USASOC	KIA 2/21/1991 Saudi Arabia
SSG Bruce L. Miller - ODA 345	Died 9/14/1991 Key West, FL
1SG Harvey L. Moore - C/1/75	Died 10/29/1992 Salt Lake City, Utah
MSG Timothy L. Martin - HHC, USASOC	Died 10/3/1993 Mogadishu, Somalia

SFC Matthew L. Rierson - HHC, USASOC	KIA 10/6/1993 Mogadishu, Somalia
LTC Craig T. Robinson - HHC, USASOC	Died 9/14/1994 Seoul, Korea
SSG Todd A. Chittenden - A/1/10 SFG(A)	Died 12/8/1994 Germany
SRA Jason C. Kutscher - 38th ARRS Sqn	Died 10/10/1994 Korea
MSG David K. Thuma - ODA 385	Died 6/18/1998 Kenya
A1C Justin C. Wotasik - 66th Rescue Sqn	Died 9/3/1998 Nellis AFB, NV
MSG Samuel B. Foster - HHC, USASOC	Died 10/3/1998 Tucson, AZ
MAJ Wallace C. Hogan - Dept of the Army, G3	KIA 9/11/2001 Pentagon
SFC Nathan R. Chapman - 3/1 SFG (A)	KIA 1/4/2002 Afghanistan
SSGT Juan M. Ridout - 320th STS	KIA 2/22/2002 Philippines
MSGT William L. McDaniel - 320th STS	KIA 2/22/2002 Philippines
SRA Jason D. Cunningham - 38th Rescue Sqn	KIA 3/4/2002 Afghanistan
TSGT John A. Chapman - 24th STS	KIA 3/4/2002 Afghanistan

MSG Peter P. Tycz - 3rd SFG(A)	KIA 6/12/2002 Afghanistan
SFC Christopher J. Speer - HHC, USASOC	KIA 8/6/2002 Afghanistan
MAJ Panuk P. Soomsawadi - SOCSOUTH	Died 8/7/2002 Puerto Rico
MSG Michael H. Maltz - 38th Rescue Sqn	KIA 3/23/2003 Afghanistan
SRA Jason T. Plite - 38th Rescue Sqn	KIA 3/23/2003 Afghanistan
SSGT Scott D. Sather - 24th STS	KIA 4/8/2003 Iraq
SFC Christopher R. Willoughby - H/121st INF (ABN)	KIA 6/20/2003 Iraq
SFC Mitchell A. Lane - C/2/3 SFG(A)	KIA 8/29/2003 Afghanistan
MSG Kevin N. Morehead - ODA 585	KIA 9/12/2003 Iraq
1LT David R. Bernstein - 1/508 PIR	KIA 10/18/2003 Iraq
MSG Kelly L. Hornbeck - 3/10 SFG(A)	KIA 1/18/2004 Iraq
SFC Robert K. McGee – ODA 155	Died 7/1/2004 Philippines

CPT Michael Y. Tarlavsky – A/1/5 SFG(A)	KIA 8/12/2004 Iraq
CPT Luke C. Wullenwaber – 1/506 IN	KIA 11/16/2004 Iraq
CPT Derek M. Argel – 23rd STS	KIA 5/30/2005 Iraq
CPT Jeremy J. Fresques – 23rd STS	KIA 5/30/2005 Iraq
SSGT Casey Crate – 23rd STS	KIA 5/30/2005 Iraq
MSG Robert M. Horrigan – HHC, USASOC	KIA 6/17/2005 Iraq
LT Michael M. McGreevy (SEAL Team 10)	KIA 6/28/2005 Afghanistan
SFC Lance S. Cornett - HHC, USASOC	KIA 2/3/2006 Iraq
SFC Chad A. Gonsalves - 3/7/SFG(A)	KIA 2/13/2006 Afghanistan
MSG Thomas D. Maholic – 2/7SFG(A)	KIA 6/24/2006 Afghanistan
SRA Adam P. Servais – 23rd STS	KIA 8/19/2006 Afghanistan
SGT Timothy P. Padgett – 1/7 SFG(A)	KIA 5/8/2007 Afghanistan
SGT Charles L. Glenn – C/2/5 SFG(A)	Died 5/15/2007 Key West, FL

SSG Joseph F. Curreri – B/2/1 SFG(A)	Died 10/27/2007 Philippines
1LT Nick A. Dewhirst – 2/506 IN	KIA 7/20/2008 Afghanistan
SGM Jerry D. Patton – USSOCOM	Died 10/15/2008 MFF DZ, Ft. Bliss, TX
SSGT Timothy P. Davis – 23rd STS	KIA 2/20/2009 Afghanistan
SSG Mark M. Maierson – A/3/7 SFG(A)	Died 3/13/2009 Key West, FL
SFC Severin W. Summers – ODA 2065	KIA 8/2/2009 Afghanistan
CPT John L. Hallett – 1/17 IN	KIA 8/25/2009 Afghanistan
SFC Shawn P. McCloskey – B/3/7 SFG(A)	KIA 9/15/2009 Afghanistan
TSGT Andrew W. Harvell – 24th STS	KIA 8/6/2011 Afghanistan
P01 Christopher Campbell – NSW Dev. Group	KIA 8/6/2011 Afghanistan
SSGT Daniel L. Zerbe – 24th STS	KIA 8/6/2011 Afghanistan
TSGT John W. Brown – 24th STS	KIA 8/6/2011 Afghanistan
SFC Aaron A. Henderson – A/2/5th SFG(A)	KIA 10/2/2012 Afghanistan

SFC Alex Viola – B/3/7SFG(A)	KIA 11/2013 Afghanistan
TSGT Michael P. Flores – 48th Rescue Sqn	KIA 6/9/2010 Afghanistan
SSG Scott R. Studenmund – B/1/5th SFG(A)	KIA 6/9/2014 Afghanistan
SSG David J. Whitcher – C/2/7 SFG(A)	Died 11/2/2016 Key West, FL
SSG James F. Moriarty – C/1/5 SFG(A)	KIA 11/4/2016 Jordan
SSG Kevin J. McEnroe – A/3/5 SFG(A)	KIA 11/4/2016 Jordan
SGM James G. "Ryan" Sartor – ODA 0225	KIA 7/13/2019 Afghanistan
SSG Micah E. Walker – A/2/10 SFG(A)	Died 7/29/2021 Key West, FL

Printed in the USA
CPSIA information can be obtained
at www.ICGtesting.com
LVHW041145290724
786631LV00003B/13